𝔖𝔱𝔲𝔡𝔦𝔢𝔰 𝔬𝔫 𝔅𝔦𝔟𝔩𝔦𝔠𝔞

No. I.

BABYLONIAN INFLUENCE ON THE BIBLE

AND POPULAR BELIEFS:

"TĔHÔM AND TIÂMAT," "HADES AND SATAN."

A COMPARATIVE STUDY OF
GENESIS I. 2.

BY

A. SMYTHE PALMER, D.D.,

AUTHOR OF "A MISUNDERSTOOD MIRACLE," "FOLK-ETYMOLOGY,"
"THE WORD-HUNTER'S NOTE-BOOK," ETC.

VICAR OF HOLY TRINITY, HERMON HILL, WANSTEAD.

LONDON:

DAVID NUTT, 270–271, STRAND.

1897.

Original © 1897
David Nutt, London

Babylonian Influence on the Bible and Popular Beliefs
ISBN 1-58509-000-X

©2000
THE BOOK TREE
All Rights Reserved

Published by
The Book Tree
Post Office Box 724
Escondido, CA 92033

We provide controversial and educational products to help awaken the public to new ideas and information that would not be available otherwise. We carry over 1100 Books, Booklets, Audio, Video, and other products on Alchemy, Alternative Medicine, Ancient America, Ancient Astronauts, Ancient Civilizations, Ancient Mysteries, Ancient Religion and Worship, Angels, Anthropology, Anti-Gravity, Archaeology, Area 51, Assyria, Astrology, Atlantis, Babylonia, Townsend Brown, Christianity, Cold Fusion, Colloidal Silver, Comparative Religions, Crop Circles, The Dead Sea Scrolls, Early History, Electromagnetics, Electro-Gravity, Egypt, Electromagnetic Smog, Michael Faraday, Fatima, Fluoride, Free Energy, Freemasonry, Global Manipulation, The Gnostics, God, Gravity, The Great Pyramid, Gyroscopic Anti-Gravity, Healing Electromagnetics, Health Issues, Hinduism, Human Origins, Jehovah, Jesus, Jordan Maxwell, John Keely, Lemuria, Lost Cities, Lost Continents, Magick, Masonry, Mercury Poisoning, Metaphysics, Mythology, Occultism, Paganism, Pesticide Pollution, Personal Growth, The Philadelphia Experiement, Philosophy, Powerlines, Prophecy, Psychic Research, Pyramids, Rare Books, Religion, Religious Controversy, Roswell, Walter Russell, Scalar Waves, SDI, John Searle, Secret Societies, Sex Worship, Sitchin Studies, Smart Cards, Joseph Smith, Solar Power, Sovereignty, Space Travel, Spirituality, Stonehenge, Sumeria, Sun Myths, Symbolism, Tachyon Fields, Templars, Tesla, Theology, Time Travel, The Treasury, UFOs, Underground Bases, World Control, The World Grid, Zero Point Energy, and much more. Call **(800) 700-TREE** for our *FREE BOOK TREE CATALOG* or visit our website at www.thebooktree.com for more information.

INTRODUCTION

Many scholars now know that the Bible creation stories had their origins in far older tales. These stories match the Old Testament stories almost identically and come from clay tablets discovered in ancient Sumeria and Babylonia. These tablets used the oldest form of writing known on earth and are the oldest preserved stories the world has ever known. They were passed down over many centuries before being adopted by Moses or whoever wrote the Old Testament.

A number of interesting concepts within these stories were carried over in the Bible from that time forward. For example, the Hebrews have a serpent who introduces mankind to sin and disobedience, which is quite likely the same dragon-serpent in the Babylonian creation story that represents physical evil and chaos. The Babylonian home for evil was in the Deep, or the Abyss, which later became transformed into Hades, or Hell.

Palmer includes a great deal of information on the dragon, whose home was in the Abyss in Babylonian literature. This dragon ultimately became the devil to later Christians. This is fascinating material and the more one explores it, the more things add up and make sense. Palmer explores the Old Testament very carefully in this work, and the Babylonian parallels are amazing.

This is a great companion book to the actual creation legends, available word for word in another set of books called *Enuma Elish*, also published by The Book Tree. With these books studied together it becomes immensely clear that the "Word of God" may not have come in its entirety directly from God, but rather "the gods". The implications on our religious beliefs and institutions would change drastically if enough people go back to the actual sources—the earliest known sources—of our beliefs systems and examine the evidence. A larger understanding is bound to result. That was the purpose Palmer had in mind when putting this book together and it is with that hope that we make it available.

Paul Tice

THE CONFLICT OF MERODACH, THE GOD OF LIGHT, WITH TIÁMAT, THE DRAGON OF CHAOS (see pp. 17, 35).

(From the Original in the British Museum)

CONTENTS

		PAGE
THE BABYLONIAN CRADLE-LAND		I
TĚHÔM AND TIÂMAT		4
THE CREATION		8
THE PRIMEVAL CHAOS		10
CONFLICT BETWEEN TIÂMAT AND MERODACH		14
THE SERPENT		23
DRAGONS OF THE BIBLE		37
THE SEA A REBELLIOUS POWER		41
THE WATERY HADES—TARTAROS		48
THE DEEP AS HELL		55
PUNISHMENT OF THE REBEL HOST		62
THE ABYSS		66
DESERTS AS THE HAUNTS OF DEVILS		72
THE EUPHRATES AS A SPIRIT RIVER		76
CONCLUSION		80
APPENDIX A.	PHENOMENAL DRAGONS	87
,, B.	MERODACH AND THE THUNDERBOLT	98
,, C.	THE SOLAR CONFLICT	106
,, D.	THE SERPENT ORACULAR	106
,, E.	NEPTUNE SATANIC	109
,, F.	"TĚHÔM"	109
,, G.	THE SPIRIT-DEEP	109
,, H.	OUR DEBT TO BABYLON	110

TEXTS ILLUSTRATED

	PAGE
Gen. i. 2 .	4, 8, 24, 66
i. 21 .	33, 41
Lev. xvi. 10	75
Deut. xxx. 13	54
Josh. xxiv. 14	3
Job vii. 12	41
ix. 13	39
xxvi. 5-6	53
xxvi. 12, 13	38, 56
xxxviii. 8-11	42
xxxviii. 16-17	53
xli. 31	51
xli. 34	57
Psalm xviii. 4	72
xxii. title	100
xl. 4	39
lxxi. 20	53
lxxiv. 13	38
civ. 9	42
cxxxix. 8-10	54
Prov. viii. 25-29	42
Isa. xiii. 22	75
xxiv. 21, 22	63
xxvii. 1	38, 57
xxxiv. 14	75
xlv. 18	11
li. 9	39

	PAGE
Jer. v. 22	43
l. 34	35
Ezek. xxix. 3	37
xxxii. 2	37
Dan. vii. 2-7	35
Amos ix. 3	39
Jonah ii. 6, 7	44
iii. 3-6	52
Esther, Additions, x. 7	36
xi. 6-11	36
Bel and the Dragon, v. 23	34
St. Matt. xii. 40	52
xii. 43	76
St. Mark iv. 39	60
St. Luke viii. 31	67
Acts xvi. 16	108
Rom. x. 7	54
2 Cor. vi. 15	72
2 Pet. ii. 4	12, 65
Jude 6	12, 65
Rev. ix. 11	68
ix. 14	76
xii. 3	69
xii. 9	28, 70
xviii. 2	75
xx. 13	67
xxii. 1	47

BABYLONIAN INFLUENCE ON THE
BIBLE AND POPULAR BELIEFS

THE "Higher Criticism," whatever mistakes it may have made in details, has at least obtained this clear result, that the human or subjective element in the Bible is now more fully recognised than heretofore. Inspiration is proved to be not so much the mechanical conveyance of new ideas and unknown facts to a passive automaton whose business is to register the revelation, as a certain divine influence which directs human researches and assimilates human modes of thought, freeing them from error, elevating them to a higher spiritual level, and utilising them for the impartation of divine truth. "First that which is natural, then that which is spiritual." God's word to man, if it is to be intelligible, must come in terms of humanity. Speaking to Hebrews, He must clothe His revelation in such figures of speech and familiar modes of thought as would be level to the Hebrew understanding.[1] And they, like every other people,

---

[1] See E. Huntingford, *Popular Misconceptions about the first Eleven Chapters of Genesis*, p. 29.

had an historic evolution; they had their own limitations and superstitions, the inherited traditions and folk-tales of a misty past, which must inevitably have coloured and reacted upon their religious beliefs. This we find to be the case. The forefather of the Jewish Church, the first who bore the name of Hebrew, came out of Harran and Ur of the Chaldees, two strongholds of the ancient Babylonian faith. Up to a certain age, while he dwelt on the other side of the Euphrates, Abraham worshipped the gods of Babylonia, as his fathers had done before him (Josh. xxiv. 2), and he never quite divested himself of the ideas in which he had been brought up, with which his mind had been tinged from infancy.[1] He could not fail to be familiar with the stories of the Creation, of Paradise, and of the Deluge, which were widely current amongst the Babylonians.[2] Al Kindy, writing about the year 830 A.D., mentions a Moslem tradition that "Abraham lived with his people fourscore years and ten in the land of Harrân, worshipping none other than Al Ozza, an idol famous in that land and adored by the men of Harrân, under the name of the Moon [i.e., Sin], which same custom prevails among them to the present day."[3]   The

---

[1] e.g., in the matter of human sacrifices, see Tomkins, *Studies on the Times of Abraham*, p. 23.   Also Delitzsch, *New Comm. on Genesis*, i. 64; Tomkins, 9.   The name Abramu is actually found in some Assyrian inscriptions (Sayce-Smith, *Chald. Genesis*, 317).

[2] E. Schrader, *Cuneiform Inscriptions and Old Test.*, i. p. xix.; Renan, *Hist. of People of Israel*, i. pp. 62–65.

[3] *Apology of Al Kindy* (ed. Muir), p. 17.

language spoken by Abraham was that of his father, Terah, the Babylonian or Assyrian, which was near akin to the Canaanitish and Hebrew tongue.[1] Therefore, when he migrated into the land of Canaan, he did not find himself altogether among strangers. He met there a people already imbued with a certain amount of Babylonian culture and literature, as the Tel el-Amarna tablets indicate,[2] and acquainted with the same gods—Nebo, Sin, Rimmon, Moloch, Anath and Ishtar—to which his fathers and himself had once been devoted.[3] The worship of some of these deities lingered even among the Israelites, we are told, down to the time of Joshua (Josh. xxiv. 14). Thus, through contact with the early inhabitants of Palestine, the Hebrews would meet anew with the religious beliefs and traditions of their Babylonian forefathers. At a later period their Samaritan neighbours, who were essentially Assyrians, would no doubt have an indirect influence in a similar direction, and their seventy years' captivity in the cradle-land of their race could not fail to revive the fading impressions of its childhood. At all events, Moses, or the compiler of the Book of Genesis, whoever he may have been, manifests a familiar

[1] Delitzsch, *New Comm. on Genesis*, ii. 197.
[2] Sayce, *Expos. Times*, vii. 265.
[3] Sayce, *Higher Criticism and the Monuments*, 79. "In the Canaan which was conquered by the Israelites we must expect to find not only Babylonian gods and forms of faith, but also Babylonian traditions, Babylonian beliefs, and Babylonian legends" (Id. 81).

acquaintance with the religious epics of Babylonia, which go back to the twenty-third century B.C., to a date, *i.e.*, about 800 years earlier than the reputed time of Moses. By being worked into these early Hebrew documents, Babylonian ideas were ensured persistence and obtained a world-wide currency. Some of these very interesting survivals we propose to examine and trace to their origin in the present essay. The first to which we will direct our attention is the evolution in Jewish thought of the spirit of evil. Very little concerning Satan, " The Enemy," is revealed in the Old Testament Scriptures ; in only four distinct passages is he explicitly mentioned.[1] Whatever conceptions, therefore, the Jews formed about his nature and character did not come so much from direct revelation as from the traditional ideas which they had inherited from their original home in the valley of the Euphrates. The *existence* of this mysterious being, it need hardly be said, is a distinct question which does not occupy us here.

1. **Tĕhôm and Tiâmat.**—We will begin by concentrating our attention on the second verse of the first chapter of Genesis, which says: " The earth was waste and void, and *darkness was upon the face of the Deep.*" The last word here is one with a history which has played an important part in the

---

[1] *Bible Dict.*, iii. 1143 ; *cf.* H. E. Ryle, *Early Narratives of Genesis*, 56 ; A. Reville, *The Devil, his Origin, Greatness and Decadence* ; J. R. Beard, *Autobiography of Satan* ; F. T. Hall, *Pedigree of the Devil ;* Roskoff, *Geschichte der Teufels.*

development of religious thought. It stands out, like an eocene boulder, amid a stratum of a later and different formation—a veritable survival from prehistoric antiquity. The word in the original is Tĕhôm, which is understood by Hebraists to be a derivative from *hûm*, to roar or rage, and so of onomatopœic origin,[1] indicating the roaring of "the deep-mouthed sea," just as Dryden speaks of the "*hoaming* sea," and Milton of the "*humming* tide."[2] Tĕhôm, then, denotes the raging water of the dark chaotic deep, which held undisputed sway over the yet unformed earth.

> "The vast immeasurable abyss
> Outrageous as a sea, dark, wasteful, wild,
> Up from the bottom turn'd by furious winds
> And surging waves, as mountains, to assault
> Heaven's height, and with the centre mix the pole."

It is to be noticed that in the Hebrew Tĕhôm is construed without the article, which would seem to

---

[1] Somewhat similarly a swell of the sea on our East Coast is sometimes called a *home* in dialect (E. Fitzgerald, *East Anglian*, iii. 1869). That the initial syllable, however, is organic is evident from its cognate Assyrian word *ti'âmtu, tâmtu* (Fried. Delitzsch, *Hebrew and Assyrian*, 66).

[2] *Lycidas*, l. 157 (1st ed. 1638 ; later editions, "whelming"). Compare Icel. *humr*, the sea ; Chinese *ho*, a river, so called from its sound ; "the great *Hou-hou*," a French popular term for the sea (Sébillot, *Légendes de la Mer*, 1886, i. 28) ; Tennyson's "moanings of the homeless sea" (*In Mem.* xxxv.) ; Kiel, *Min. Prophets*, ii. 107 ; Farrar, *Chapters on Lang.*, 26.

[3] *Paradise Lost*, vii. 211-215.

imply that it is an old traditional name for that
which had partly been personified and mythologised,
as if in English, instead of writing "the deep," we
gave the word a capital—"Darkness was upon the
face of Deep (or Chaos)." And this personification
at an earlier stage had really been made.[1] The
Hebrew cosmogony contains, beyond question, some
mythic elements of a very archaic type, of which one
of the most notable here presents itself. These
elements, it is admitted on all sides, are of Babylonian
origin. The ancient legends of the Creation which
were current in Mesopotamia before the dawn of
history were assimilated by the inspired writer, but
in such a manner that the mythological and poly-
theistic element in them was carefully discarded, and
a purely monotheistic element substituted in its
place.[2] In this particular instance the Semitic
Tĕhôm, "Deep," of Genesis accurately corresponds
to the synonymous Assyrian word Tiâmat, frequently met with on the cuneiform tablets and
monuments. Tiâmat was the great watery abyss
which was the ultimate source of all created things.
As the fourth tablet of the Creation story expresses it:

The expression "*face* of Deep" is not to be urged in this
connection, although a picture in the Cathedral of Monreale
(thirteenth century) represents the primeval water with an actual
countenance, over which the dove is moving (Jameson and
Eastlake, *History of our Lord*, i. 78).

[2] Cheyne and Jensen, *Critical Review*, v. 261.

"The primeval [1] Deep was their generator,
  Mummu Tiâmat [Chaos Deep] was the mother of them all."[2]

This watery waste, Tiâmat, which at first covered the earth, afterwards came to be conceived as the ocean stream that encircled it,[3] which led to further developments. It contained within it the germs of the whole universe:

" The earth was form'd, but in the womb as yet
  Of waters, embryon immature involved,
  Appear'd not ; over all the face of earth
  Main ocean flow'd, not idle." [4]

In South Babylonia this " matter unformed and void " was known under the name of Bahu, " the great mother, the generatress of mankind." [5]   Bahu, the deep of chaos, where the seven evil spirits or storm demons have their home, is evidently only another aspect of Tiâmat.   It is the original of the Hebrew bohû, which, in the verse of Genesis we are considering, appears in the formula tohû vabohû, " waste and desolation."   In the Phœnician cosmogony it appears as Baau, the mother of the first man.   In these ancient cosmologies Tiâmat or Bohu,

---

[1] Assyr. rishtû corresponding exactly to Heb. rêshith, beginning Gen. i. 1 (Rev. C. J. Ball).

[2] Sayce, Religion of Ancient Babylonians, Hibbert Lectures, 1887. p. 384 ; Boscawen, Bible and the Monuments, 42, 45 ; Tiele would identify Egyptian tûau, the abyss, with Tiâmat (History of Religion, 58) ; but tian, the deep, as cited by Delitzsch, seems a closer parallel (New Comm. on Gen., ii. 264).

[3] Sayce, Hib. Lect., 374-5, 391.   [4] Paradise Lost, vii. 276-279.

[5] Sayce, Hib. Lect., 449.   The Icelandic account of primordial chaos in the Völuspa has several points of agreement.

the watery abyss, was the primal source[1] of the universe. This chaos was the first thing that existed, and out of it earth and sky were formed. To symbolise this fact huge brazen lavers termed "abysses" (*apsu*), were ritually employed in Babylonian temples, and even in Solomon's temple the "sea" which he made of molten metal had the same meaning.[2]   Here, also, is evidently the origin of the Buthos, or unfathomable deep, which the Gnostic Valentinus held to be the self-existent first principle from which all the æons of his system emanated.[3]

2. **The Account of the Creation.**—In Genesis no account is given of the absolute *Creation* of the world, but only of the formation of the Kosmos, the established order of nature as it now exists. In verses 1 and 2 we find a primordial matter or

---

[1] Compare the pre-creation "water's fathomless abyss" of the Rig-Veda (M. Müller, *Hist. of Sansk. Lit.*, 564); the watery chaos of Pherecydes (Lenormant, *Beginnings of History*, 540); and that of the Mexicans (D. G. Brinton, *Myths of the New World*, 129); Hesiod, *Theog.*, l. 116 *seq.* In the Vedas the waters are the mothers of creation (H. W. Wallis, *Cosmology of the Rig-Veda*, 56-58). Smith, *Chald. Genesis*, 1880, 60; K. S. Macdonald, *The Vedic Religion,* 129.

[2] Sayce, *Hib. Lect.*, 63 ; *Expos. Times*, vii. 264.

[3] Hippolytus, *Refut. of Heresies*, I. xxv. ; Irenæus, I. i. Tertullian, not understanding this, censures the Valentinian use of Bythos as a name most unfit for one who dwells in the heights above (*Contra Val.*, vii.). Referring, however, to Gen. i. 2, he says : "Habes homo imprimis aetatem venerari aquarum, quod antiqua substantia."—*De Baptismo*, cap. iii. See also C. W. King, *The Gnostics*, 26, 37.

"stuff" already in existence as a presupposed fact. The Spirit of God, or possibly the Wind of God, or a potent wind (the word for Spirit and Wind being the same in Hebrew), is represented as hovering with a gentle birdlike motion over the dark surging waters of Těhôm, the primal flood, and under its fostering influence the work of creation goes forward peacefully and harmoniously. As Milton paraphrases it with sufficient accuracy:

> " His brooding wings the Spirit of God outspread,
> And vital virtue infused and vital warmth,
> Throughout the fluid mass." [1]

Professor Tiele observes that the Egyptians regarded four pairs of cosmic powers as taking part in the work of creation in a manner closely analogous to the Semitic representation. " In endless duration (Heh and Heht = Assyr. *rishtû*, Heb. *rêshith*)

---

[1] *Paradise Lost*, vii. 235-237. Very similarly Sylvester:

> " As a hen that fain would hatch a brood
> Sits close thereon, and with her lively heat
> Of yellow-white bals doth lyve birds beget:
> Even in such sort seemed the Spirit Eternall
> To brood upon this gulf."

(*Div. Weekes and Workes*, 1621, p. 8.)

The Indians of the New World conceived that Hurakan, the mighty fertilising wind, passed over the waters of Chaos in the form of a huge bird, and so called the earth into being (D. G. Brinton, *Myths of the New World*, 210 *seq*.). The Finnish Kalevala has the same idea. Compare the myths of the world-egg. The account of the Creation given in the Rig-Veda (*Mand.*, x. 129) has many points in common (see M. Williams, *Hinduism*, 26).

was darkness (Kek and Kekt) on the abyss (Nun and Nunt = Tĕhôm), and the waters of this primeval ocean were moved by the wind (Neni and Nenit), the breath of the deity." [1] The Babylonian account of creation, however, was conceived in a very different spirit. Here Tiâmat, the dark aboriginal chaos, is regarded as no part of the Divine creation, but as a self-determining, brutal power disowning the authority of Anu, the god of heaven. The process of reducing this elemental savage into law and order takes the form of a violent struggle or conflict between Merodach, the creator and mediator, the son of Anu, "the god of the good (or refreshing) wind," [2] deputed for this purpose, and Tiâmat, depicted as a resisting and antagonistic monster. Creation is the subjugation of this unreclaimed brute force, and the instruments with which Merodach arms himself for the encounter are the winds.

3. **The Primeval Chaos.**—We have seen that the notion of the chaos of darkness and disorder coming *as such* from the hands of the heavenly Creator found no acceptance with the Babylonian cosmographer. It could not but be a difficulty to a thoughtful mind. If we hold that the material substratum of the Kosmos was created in the first instance a confused and formless conglomerate, a *tohú vabohú*, *i.e.*, a desolate and unorganised mass, we have to suppose that this *imperfect* creation was

---

[1] *Hist. of Religion*, 49, 50.
[2] Pinches, *Relig. Ideas of the Babylonians* (Vic. Inst.), 5.

a rude and tentative beginning, a preparatory and provisional means to a subsequent end. This seems so unlikely in itself, and so little consonant with the Divine way of working—for God is not the author of confusion (1 Cor. xiv. 33)—that many have sought to escape from the difficulty by regarding the detailed account given in the First of Genesis as not that of the original creation, but rather that of the recreation or reconstruction of a material world already existent, and already, for some unexplained reason, brought to confusion. The prophet Isaiah states explicitly that God " created not the earth a *tohu* or desolation " (xlv. 18), and, in this view, there is nothing contradictory when Genesis says, as it apparently does, that the earth which God had created " in the beginning " (v. 1) had " *become* desolation and emptiness " (v. 2).[1]

How then did the earth come to have fallen from its original state, which we may be sure was good, into the chaotic condition represented in the opening verses of Genesis? Kurtz and others [2] have conjectured with much reason that between the first and second verses must be read in the fall of Satan and his rebel angels, and that some such catastrophe appears to be hinted by the words employed. As a defective creation is hardly conceivable, there must

---

[1] See McCaul, *Aids to Faith*, 208; Delitzsch, *New Comm. on Genesis*, i. 79, 80.

[2] *e.g.*, Stier and Baumgarten ; see also G. S. Faber, *The Many Mansions*, 279, 280 ; Lange, *Life of Christ*, ii. 46.

have been some hostile power at work which had introduced ruin and desolation into what had originally been the perfect handiwork of the Almighty. Inasmuch then as the words *tohû rabohû*, when used in other passages of scripture (*e.g.*, Isa. xxxiv. 11; Jer. iv. 23), imply not mere negative imperfection, but actual laying waste and positive desolation, so, it is thought, they must denote here traces of wreck and ruin which had been wrought in the earth by the overthrow of its original denizens, the angels who, by rebelling against God, kept not their first estate, but left their own habitation (Jude 6; 2 Pet. ii. 4), and were cast down into the abyss. "That old first darkness of which Moses speaks in the second verse of scripture,"[1] says Stier, "God, the father of lights and of light, did not create. He could never have said, 'Let there be darkness!' Darkness is the product and witness of the first apostasy in the light-heaven of the first creation . . . Through sin the below and the abyss [*i.e.*, Tiâmat] have come into being."[2] To the same purport Baumgarten : "The apostasy of the spirits [to whom the earth was given at the beginning] had its consequence in the devastation, the darkening, the dominion of the roaring abyss [*i.e.*, Tiâmat] on the

---

[1] The Arabs have a word for chaos, the waters under the earth, the sea, cognate with Heb. *ôlâm*, time of old, the dark backward and abyss of time (Hommel, *Proc. Soc. Bib. Arch.* xvii. 201).

[2] *Comm. on Ep. of S. James* (Eng. trans.), 257.   So W. Law (Vaughan, *Hours with the Mystics*).

earth, as the territory and sphere appointed for these spirits." [1]   Accordingly the Mosaic account of the six days' creation would really have to do with the reconstruction of the marred and disorganised earth, which the Creator reduced to order after the banishment of the fallen angels. [2]

With this may be compared the Babylonian legend of the revolt of a portion of the heavenly host.   In the fourth book of the Creation-Epic Bel (Merodach) challenges Tiâmat with the words " Trouble on high thou hast excited " (Sayce, " Higher Criticism," 67). They also had arrived at the opinion, held by many commentators, [3] that it was in order to restore the disturbed harmony of the universe, and to fill up the gap left by the defection of the rebel angels, that mankind were created :

> " A better race to bring
> Into their vacant room." [4]

One of the Creation tablets says that Merodach, the Creator, " caused the yoke to be laid on the gods

---

[1] *Apostolic History*, iii. 152.

[2] Kurtz, *Hist. of the Old Covenant*, i. pp. xxvi.–xxviii., lvi., lxii.–lxiv. We cannot follow him into his speculation that the serpent and the tree of Knowledge—both deadly and diabolic instruments—were permitted to stand over in the renewed earth as survivals of the previous state of cosmic evil. See also Lenormant, *Beginnings of History*, 104.   The N. A. Indian legends similarly treat the Creation as the mere reconstruction of a world overwhelmed by the primeval ocean (D. G. Brinton, *Myths of the New World*, 213).

[3] *e.g.*, Kurtz, i. p. lvii.

[4] *Paradise Lost*, vii. 190, and similarly, ix. 147–149.

[angels] who were his enemies, and on account of their sin created mankind,"[1] or, as M. Oppert translates it, " To form a counterpoise to them the god of life created mankind."[2] The Revolt in Heaven tablet has been translated as follows:

" To those rebel angels [*ili*, gods] He prohibited return ;
He stopped their service ; He removed them unto the gods [*ili*] who were His enemies.
In their room He created Mankind.
The first who received life dwelt with Him.
May He give them strength never to neglect His word,
According to the voice of the serpent[3] whom His hands had made."[4]

4. Conflict between Tiâmat and Merodach.

—From what has been said we can see that Tiâmat, the chaos of the great deep, came to be regarded as the manifestation of enmity to heaven and its ruler, and even as itself a hostile and resisting power which the good Creator had to subdue and force into submission. Tiâmat, accordingly, was

[1] Pinches, *Relig. Ideas of the Babylonians* (Vic. Inst.), p. 5.
[2] Schrader, *Cuneiform Insc. and Old Text.*, i. 26 ; "In their room" (Talbot, *Records of Past*, vii. 127).
[3] "The crowned one"—*i.e.* the βασιλίσκος (?).
[4] Fox Talbot, *Trans. Soc. Bib. Arch.*, iv. 251-2. So Baur, " Man is and signifies that other host which God created instead of Lucifer's host expelled from Lucifer's place"; see Lange (*Life of Christ*, ii. 46), who holds a similar view, and thinks that Satan's present Spirit-Kingdom bears traces of a shattered earthly kingdom anterior to man, and stands in a cosmical relation to a ruined prehuman world (id. p. 43). Compare S. Luke iv. 6; S. John xii. 31 ; Eph. vi. 12.

personified as a hideous female monster [1] attended by a brood of evil and misshapen creatures. She is the great dragon of darkness, with which the god of light, Merodach, engages in deadly conflict. Inasmuch, then, as Tiâmat is the ideal representative of all disorder, anarchy and chaos, to counteract and vanquish her is to bring order out of confusion, to educe the beautiful Kosmos and the regular course of nature out of a " rudis indigestaque moles." [2] It is, in the words of Carlyle, " a mighty conquest over chaos." Thus to the poetical mind of the Babylonian the divine work of creation appeared as a noble victory [3] gained by the good spirit over brute matter, by light over the power of darkness ; and he depicted it, first mentally and then on his monuments, as a terrific struggle between the kindly sun-god and the dragon of disorder. Merodach, the benignant deity who is the special mediator and benefactor of mankind, is appointed by Anu, the supreme god, as champion of the heavenly powers, to do battle with the evil monster. Long and terrible was the conflict that ensued. [4] Tiâmat, as a rampant dragon, lifted

---

[1] *Cf.* "The Deep (Tehôm) that coucheth beneath" (Deut. xxxiii. 13), in the attitude of a crouching wild beast (Gen. xlix. 9). Appendix, note A.

[2] Ovid, *Met.*, i. 7. Compare a fine passage in Martineau, *Endeavours after the Christian Life* (6th ed.), p. 389.

[3] So the *Beowulf* says of the Creator that He
> " *Victorious* [sige-hrôðig] set the sun and the moon
> As lights for light to the land-dwellers," ll. 94–5.

Sayce, *Hib. Lect.*, 378 ; *Expos. Times*, vii. 207 ; Maspero

herself up with extended wings and tore at her opponent with tooth and claw, with jaws gaping wide as if to swallow him; but Merodach, raising on high the thunderbolts with which he was armed, thrust a storm-wind down her throat, which caused the monster to burst in sunder; and then the demons which were with her fled in dismay from before the victorious god. A very graphic description of this duel, in which the celestial champion overthrew "the scaly Tiâmat," is given on one of the Assyrian tablets, of which a rendering by Rev. C. J. Ball here follows in a condensed form. Speaking of Merodach it says:

"A weapon[1] his right hand he made grasp . . .
He shot lightning with his countenance.
He made a net[2] to throw round the monster Tiâmat . . .
The four winds he seized . . .
He created a storm-wind, a baleful wind, a hurricane, a
    whirlwind . . .
The monster Tiâmat, coiling herself, cometh after him;
The Lord also raised the flood, his mighty weapon;

Dawn of Civilisation, 538–542 (2nd ed.); Gunkel, *Schöpfung und Chaos*, p. 111.

[1] *Saparu*, the sickle-shaped sword, thought to represent the lightning (Smith, *Chald. Genesis*, 109). See R. Brown, *The Unicorn*, 52–54. The Bulgarians say of the midsummer sun that on St. John's Day he dances and *whirls swords* about, *i.e.*, sends out piercing, dazzling rays (Ralston, *Songs of Russ. People*, 242).

[2] This net is illustrated by a stele discovered by M. de Sarsec. The figure of a god carries under its right arm a net containing a number of captives entangled in its meshes (*Quarterly Review*, vol. clxxix. p. 349). *Cf.* Hab. i. 15.

That chariot which levelleth all enemies he rode . . .
Then Tiâmat assailed the prince of the gods, Merodach ;
In battle she came on, she closed in conflict.
The Lord also spread his net, he threw it round her ;
A storm-wind, taking the rear, before him he let loose.
Tiâmat opened her mouth to draw it in :
The storm-wind she received within her, so that she could
    not close her lips. . . .
She was pierced through the heart, and her mouth she
    opened wide.
He bound her and her life he swallowed up,
Her carcase he cast down, upon her he stood.
When Tiâmat the leader he had vanquished,
Her might he broke, her army was routed ;
And the gods her helpers, marching beside her,
Wheeled round, were terrified, turned their back . . .
. . . and their weapons he brake in pieces."[1]

In this stirring narrative Merodach is seen letting
loose the winds to conquer Tiâmat, just as in Genesis
a wind from Elohim passes over the face of Tĕhôm
to make it amenable to His wishes. No form was
too hideous to be given to that turbulent monster.
An Assyrian bas-relief representing this fierce encounter is in the British Museum, and the subject
is often repeated on Babylonian cylinders.[2] The
demon is depicted with huge talons like a bird of
prey, with fanged jaws and extended wings, with

[1] C. J. Ball, *Speaker's Comm. on the Apocrypha*, ii. 347. See
also Sayce, *Hib. Lect.*, 380–382, and a revised translation in
Higher Criticism and the Monuments. 65 *seq.* ; Jensen, *Kosmologie
der Babylonier*, 278 *seq.* and 307 *seq.*

[2] See the Oxford *Bible Illustrations*, plate cvi. The coins of
Abdera (B.C. 500–400) bear the figure of a winged griffin (Bunbury Collection, Nos. 560–571).

B

horns upon her head and a stumpy tail. She retreats
fighting before the onslaught of Merodach, the god
of light,[1] who presses her close with uplifted thunderbolts. This Babylonian conception of the power of
evil, as we shall presently see, passed into all lands.
On the ancient Persian bas-reliefs the evil-spirit,
over which the king is combating victorious, is
invariably represented as a winged monster which
bears an indubitable resemblance to the Chaldean
Tiâmat. See the figures in Perrot and Chipiez, *Art
in Persia*, pp. 145, 148, 322, 428, 455, 465. Indeed,
these grotesque monsters, wherein the shapes of birds
and beasts of prey are united and fused together, to
which the Greeks gave the name of *grypes*, griffins,[2]
are found everywhere, in Egypt, in Phœnicia and
Asia Minor, as well as in Mesopotamia (ib. 147).
Very probably of the same brood is the four-legged
winged monster by which Oceanus is borne in the
Prometheus Vinctus of Æschylus (ll. 294, 403).[3]
But a more obvious survival of Tiâmat (Thamtē)
on Greek soil is presented in Thaumas, who was
fabled to have sprung from the union of Pontus
(Sea) and Gê (Earth), and became the father of the
monstrous bird-formed Harpies (Whirlwinds) and
Iris (Rainbow) (Hesiod, *Theog.*, ll. 237, 265).[4]

---

[1] Appendix, note B.   [2] See note 2, p. 17.

[3] So the Sanskrit ocean-god Varuna is carried by a marine
monster, Makara (Goldstücker, *Lit. Remains*, i. 257).

[4] *Cf.* Ovid, *Met.* iv. 479 ; xiv. 845. Possibly Mômos (Blame,
Reproach), one of the brood of the gloomy goddess Night
(Hesiod, *Theog.*, 214), may stand for the Assyrian *Mummu* (Chaos),

It is not difficult to see what was the natural phenomenon which served as the groundwork of this earliest conception of the Creation. When the glorious sun rose out of the cold dark waters of the sea, dispelling the gloom and mists of night, in which the earth had been wrapt while silence brooded over it, and "all things were hushed as Nature's self lay dead;" as he mounted the sky, bringing life in his genial warmth, and, as it were, calling back into being all that had been buried in formless obscurity during the chill hours of darkness, it seemed to primitive man hardly less than an actual creation going on before his eyes.[1] It was the daily restoration of a dead world. The mythologising faculty everywhere regarded the rising sun going forth to his daily conflict and victory as a warrior-god, whose spear and arrows were the bright rays which he scattered around him;[2] while the dark water, over which he mounted triumphant, and the clouds of night which he put to flight, were the vanquished monsters which he destroyed, either the devouring serpent of the deep or the flying dragons of the air.

---

a name often given to Tiâmat (Sayce, *Hib. Lect.*, 384 ; Lenormant, *Chald. Magic*, 170).

[1] So in Egyptian Ra, "the Maker of Existence" (*qui facit esse*) is the sun as Revealer and Creator (Brugsch); Cook, *Origins of Religion and Language*, 448.

[2] *Cf.* "On the ridge of the hills rose the broad, bright sun
          in his glory,
      Hurling his arrows abroad on the glittering crests
          of the surges" (Kingsley, *Andromeda*).

Even a modern divine, in a sermon at Westminster, fell naturally into the same mode of expression when he spoke of "darkness still struggling with light, yet ever receding; retreating step by step, and pierced through and through as it retreats by the glittering shafts of the true king of day."[1] And Shakspere, with the primitive instinct, says :

[1] Abp. Trench, *Westminster Sermons*, p. 3.

The Syrians, in like manner, regarded Shamash, the sun, as creator and prime mover of the universe. Compare the Rig-Veda,

> " Him let us praise, the golden child that rose
> In the beginning, who was born the Lord—
> The one sole Lord of all that is—who made
> The earth and formed the sky, who giveth life . . .
> Where'er let loose in space, the mighty waters
> Have gone, depositing a fruitful seed,
> And generating fire, there *he* arose,
> Who is the breath and life of all the gods,
> Whose mighty glance looks round the vast expanse
> Of watery vapour—source of energy,
> The only God above the gods."
> (*Mand. I.*, hymn 121 ; M. Williams, *Hinduism*, 27.)

Prof. M. Müller dwells upon "The natural awe with which the earliest dwellers on the earth saw that brilliant being slowly rising from out the darkness of the night, raising itself by its own might higher and higher, till it stood triumphant on the arch of heaven, and then descended and sank down in its fiery glory into the dark abyss of the heaving and hissing sea." To the primitive man "the sunrise was the first wonder, the first beginning of all reflection, all thought, all philosophy ; it was to him the first revelation, the first beginning of all trust, of all religion " (M. Muller, *Selected Essays*, i. 600 (1881)). It was in a certain way the *cause* of all things which he beholds (ib. 604).

" Night's swift dragons cut the clouds full fast,
   And yonder shines Aurora's harbinger." [1]

" Swift, swift, you dragons of the night, that dawning
   May bare the raven's eye !" [2]

So to the ancient Egyptians the sun-god Ra, the creator, the cause of all life on earth, rose in his brightness out of the gloomy depths of the great water Nu, the primeval matter from which all things sprung,[3] in which lay bound in chains the serpent Refref, the symbol of evil, otherwise called Apap, the dragon-foe.[4] The deep seemed to gain the victory when it swallowed him up, as Osiris, in the darkening west (Set); but he is always triumphant in the morning when he comes forth as Horus or Un-nefer, " the Glorious Riser." Then Ra pierces with his weapons the serpent of darkness, Apap; or, as Horus, spears the crocodile of the watery Hades. As Khepera (another name of the rising sun) he is the type of matter passing into life, and the quickening of the dead; to him all animal and vegetable life is due.[5]

---

[1] *Midsummer Night's Dream*, iii. 2, 380.
[2] *Cymbeline*, ii. 2, 49 ; so—
   "The dragon wing of night o'erspreads the earth."
                        (*Tro. and Cress.* v. 8, 17.)
[3] Budge, *Book of the Dead*, p. xcvii.
[4] Apap or Apepi (from âp, to mount up) is said to be the thunder-cloud (Renouf).
[5] Renouf, *Religion of Ancient Egypt*, 109-113, 118 ; Budge, *Book of the Dead*, cix. 246 ; Brinton, *Essays of an Americanist*, 137-8 ; Goldziher, *Myth. among the Hebrews*, 185.

Thus the hand-to-hand encounter of the Babylonian powers of light and darkness, Merodach and Tiâmat, is the prototype and forerunner of a long series of similar conflicts in various mythologies; those, *e.g.*, between Thraêtaona and the dragon Dahâka;[1] between Mithra and Ahriman; Zeus and Typhon; Apollo and Python ; Perseus and Gorgo ; Sigurd and Fafnir; Beowulf and Grendel; St. George and the Dragon.[2] The Vedas present a striking analogy in the deadly combat between Indra, the Aryan war-god, assisted by the Maruts or Storm-winds, and the serpent Ahi or Vritra, the power of darkness, whom the god destroys with his thunderbolts.[3] So in Egypt Osiris, the sun-god, contends with Apap, the Egyptian Satan ;[4] and so in the new world, Michabo, the god of light, pierces with his dart the prince of serpents who lives in a lake and floods the earth with its waters.[5] In most mythologies dragons are popular personifications of awe-inspiring meteorological pheno-mena, such as darkness, the storm-cloud, the water-spout, the torrent or flood. (Appendix, note A.)

[1] *Zend-Avesta* (ed. Mills), iii. 233–4. Appendix, note C.

[2] Lenormant, *Beginnings of History*, 107 ; *Chald. Magic*, 232–3 ; F. E. Hulme, *Symbolism in Christ. Art*, 111 *seq.*; Baring-Gould, *Curious Myths*, 300–310.

[3] Maury, *Croyances et Légendes de l'Antiquité*, 106 *seq.* ; Ragozin, *Vedic India*, 199.

[4] Maury, 304. Compare among the Slavonians the conflict of Byelbog, the god of light, against Chernobog, the god of dark-ness (Ralston, *Songs of the Russian People*, 103).

[5] D. G. Brinton, *Myths of the New World*, 122.

5. **The Serpent.**—The dragon Tiâmat readily
came to be confused and identified with an inde-
pendent conception, the serpent of darkness, which
was itself the offspring of the great deep and an
enemy of the heavenly powers.[1] The Dragon of
Chaos, according to the tablets, was banished to
the depths of the underworld, and sometimes the
monster is described as having the body of a
woman terminating in the coiled tails of two
serpents,[2] and by a natural transition was merged
sometimes in "the evil serpent," "the monstrous
serpent of the sea," "the serpent of darkness,"
which is coiled around the earth.[3] We have here
a glimmering of the reason why the evil spirit
was conceived by the writer of Genesis as wearing

[1] A memorial-stone of Merodach Baladan I. (B.C. 1320) calls on
the infernal deities, Ea, Ninip, and Gula, "all the gods on this
stone tablet whose emblems are seen, violently to destroy the
name" of him who moves this boundary stone. Among the
emblems are the winged dragon (Tiâmat) and a horned serpent
(Smith, *Assyr. Discoveries*, 236–7). A pair of winged dragons
are sculptured on the doorway of Sennacherib's palace (ib. 308).
See also Smith, *Chald. Genesis*, 101, 113.

[2] *Cf.* the figure of the serpentine water-fay Melusina in
Pucé Church, Gironde, and that of the Babylonian mermaid
given in Baring-Gould, *Curious Myths*, pp. 470, 496 (ed. 1869).
The Irish merrow (*morûach*) is both a sea-monster and mermaid
(Croker, *Fairy Legends of South Ireland*, ed. Wright, p. 188).

[3] Boscawen, *The Bible and the Monuments*, 41, 45 ; *From
Under the Dust of Ages*, 39 ; Sayce, *Hib. Lect.*, 283. The original
religious conception, says Ewald, was of the serpent as a beast
of the abyss, fierce and fearful ; then as connected with the
dead and the under-world (*Revelation*, 226).

the form of a serpent. He introduces him, without explanation, with a prefixed article, " *the* serpent," as one already well known in the current beliefs of his people. This abrupt entrance of the serpent upon the scene, as Baumgarten remarks, seems to imply that he had stood in some relation to the earth previous to the six days' creation. " Of this relation," he says, " I find a trace in Gen. i. 2, where the earth is described as a territory of darkness, of emptiness, and of the roaring deep. In such a condition of the earth, I cannot by any means recognise the *beginning* of the ways and works of God."[1] In other words, in Tĕhôm (Tiâmat) the destructive power of evil was already manifest. Its visible incarnation was the dragon or serpent.[2] And we can trace, as Professor Sayce has suggested, in the Babylonian story the reason why the reptile was esteemed " more subtle than any other beast of the field," because it is associated there with the sea-god Ea.[3] Now Ea was not only the god of waters but the god of wisdom.[4] He had his dwelling in Absu, which denoted both the abyss or deep and the sea of knowledge. Depth and profundity have ever been synonymous with wisdom. This primeval Absu in Accadian belief was situated at the head of the Persian Gulf and at the mouth of the Euphrates, because there was for them the

[1] See also W. F. Cobb, *Origines Judaicæ*, 175.

[2] See Sayce, *Babylonian Literature*, 46.

[3] Appendix, note D.

Records of the Past, xi. 57

entrance to the deep or ocean-stream, "the ever-sounding and mysterious sea." There lay Eridu, "the good city," the original of the Eden of Genesis. There all worship and culture took its beginning. And just as the natives of our own northern isles, looking out over the dim mystic sea, imagined that they saw the immense sea-snake, the Kraken, which dwells

> "Below the thunders of the upper deep,
> Far, far beneath in the abysmal sea,"

sometimes arising out of its depths, or else a water-fay which, "mingling her voice with the sighing breeze, was often heard to sing of subterranean wonders, or to chant prophecies of future events;"[1] so the voice, which was borne to the Babylonians from the deep, seemed full of mystery, and its god, they thought, must be a god of knowledge. The watery abyss—Tiâmat in its primitive sense—was thus the home and the visible embodiment of Ea, and he was regarded as being at once the god of waters, the god of wisdom and god of the infernal region.[2] He

---

[1] Sir W. Scott, *The Pirate*, ch. ii. When Castrén asked an old Samoyede where was that higher divine power which he called Num, he at once pointed to the dark distant sea, and said : "*He is there*" (M. Müller, *Science of Religion*, 202).

[2] G. Smith, *Assyr. Discoveries*, 220. *Cf.* Proteus, the Ancient of the Deep, the prophetic old man of the sea, who knew the past, the present, and the future (Virgil, *Georg.*, iv. 393). To the ancient Irish the roaring of the sea seemed fraught with ominous and prophetic forebodings (Joyce, *Irish Names of Places*, ii. 251).

was the lord of the deep, which, like the Okeanos of Homer, was supposed as a flowing stream to surround the earth in a serpentine coil. This binding and encircling stream was called sometimes "the rope of the universe," more often it was compared to a huge snake or serpent.[1] Then by a natural transition Ea himself came to be symbolised as a serpent, and was styled "God of the river of the great snake."[1] This primeval sea-serpent is evidently identical with Tiâmat, the dragon of the great deep. One old Accadian hymn, for instance, speaks of "the strong serpent of the sea," which sweeps away the foe, another of "the sea-monsters of Chaos."[2] And as this serpent is closely connected with the god of wisdom we discern the reason without difficulty why

---

[1] Compare Icel. *Jörmungandr*, the encircling world-snake (Grimm, *Teut. Myth.*, 182), and Gerdha. "Girder," the earth-binding sea (Tiele, *Hist. of Religions*, 197, 200), and Keary, *Cont. Rev.*, Oct. 1879, p. 249. The Persian Nestorians think that the ocean stream surrounding the earth is the leviathan swimming round it (A. Grant, *The Nestorians*, 1843). The Talmud says that Chaos is a green line surrounding the whole world from which darkness proceeds (Hershon, *Talmudic Genesis*, 7). *Cf.* the Homeric Hymn to Neptune, "whose graceful green hair circles all the earth" (Chapman, p. 11, *Lib. Old Authors*). Vishnu, as Supreme God, is drawn by the infinite world-serpent ('Tesha or Ananta) over the waves of the primeval ocean (Tiele, *Hist. of Religions*, 144).

> "That sea-snake, tremendous curl'd,
> Whose monstrous circle girds the world."
>   (Scott, *Lay of the Last Minstrel*, vi. 22.)

[2] Sayce, *Hib. Lect.*, 134, 141, 282.

it is described in Genesis as the subtlest of created things.[1]

The Assyrian serpent of darkness continued in Semitic belief to be the incarnation of guile and wickedness, and became an apt emblem of the evil principle. We have seen, moreover, that this cosmic serpent of the deep was originally one with Tiâmat, the dragon leader of the powers of night and chaos.[2] Indeed, some cylinders depict Tiâmat in the form of a huge serpent when assailed in the creation-conflict[3] by Merodach. The Babylonians believed the serpent, as a beast coming out of the abyss, to be a demoniacal being—as the Arabs still call a serpent a *jinn*—and gave it also the name of Tiâmat, and sometimes *aibu*, "the enemy,"[4] which in Hebrew is the meaning of

---

[1] See Boscawen, *Bible and the Monuments*, 85-89. Accordingly with a true poetic instinct, Byron makes Cain inquire, on beholding a pre-Adamite ocean monster or leviathan,

> " Yon immense
> Serpent, which rears its dripping mane and vasty
> Head ten times higher than the haughtiest cedar
> Forth from the abyss, looking as he could coil
> Himself around the orbs we lately look'd on—
> Is he not of the kind which bask'd beneath
> The tree in Eden ? " (*Cain*, ii. 2).

Appendix, note D.

[2] Lenormant, *Chald. Magic*, 232 ; Sayce, *Hib. Lect.*, 283.

[3] The Phœnician mythology tells of a contest between Kronos and "the old Ophion" (= the old serpent of Gen. iii.) (Lenormant, *Beginnings of History*, 545-6 ; Smith, *Chald. Genesis*, 90).

[4] Delitzsch, *New Comm. on Genesis*, vol. i. ; H. E. Ryle, *Early Narratives of Genesis*, 38, 39 ; Boscawen, *Bab. and Orient. Record*, Oct. 1890.

Satan.   And the two conceptions are fundamentally and originally one.   When St. John says in the Apocalypse (xii. 9), "The great dragon was cast down, the old serpent, he that is called the Devil and Satan," there is a manifest reference to the opening chapters of Genesis and the ancient cosmogonic idea that underlies them.[1]   By the dragon in that passage is denoted a sea-monster,[2] the *tannîm* so often referred to in the Old Testament as potentate of the sea and of the dark mystic world which hides "the secrets of the hoary deep."[3]   Milton, with the divining instinct of the poet, reverts to the primeval type when he represents Satan

> " With head uplift above the wave, . . .
>   his other parts besides
> Prone on the flood, extended long and large,
> Lay floating many a rood ; in bulk as huge
>   [as] that sea-beast
> Leviathan, which God of all His works
> Created hugest that swim the ocean stream." [4]

We can trace how this curious evolution came about by help of the Babylonian religion.   Tiâmat, the raging world of waters, is there the ideal of anarchy and confusion,

---

[1] " Wheresoever thou findest disorder, there is thy eternal enemy ; attack him swiftly, subdue him ; make Order of him, the subject not of Chaos but of Intelligence, Divinity, and Thee " (Carlyle, *Past and Present*, bk. iii. ch. 12).

[2] See Hengstenberg, *in loco*.

[3] Milton, *Paradise Lost*, ii. 891.

[4] Ibid., i. 193-202.

> "A dark
> Illimitable ocean, without bound,
> Without dimension, where length, breadth, and height,
> And time, and place are lost ; where eldest Night
> And Chaos, ancestors of Nature, hold
> Eternal anarchy, amidst the noise
> Of endless wars, and by confusion stand.
>   .   .   .   This wild abyss
> The womb of Nature, and perhaps her grave—
> Of neither sea, nor shore, nor air, nor fire,
> But all these in their pregnant causes mix'd
> Confusedly, and which thus must ever fight." [1]

What wonder that this turbulent discord came to be personified as " the Evil One " by bad pre-eminence, and ".the enemy of the gods." [2] It was made to stand not only for Chaos—which was a somewhat similar personification among the Greeks (Hesiod, *Theog.*, 116, Χάος) of aboriginal confusion as a " gaping " open-mouthed monster [3]—but for all the evils and disorders that proceeded out of Chaos. In particular, it was the death-bringing serpent that first beguiled men and tempted them to sin. Thus Tiâmat, the Deep, the source of physical evil, passed by a natural transition into the Demon of Moral Evil. And, in the same way, the process of creation, conceived as a primeval conflict between Merodach and Tiâmat, or Bel and the Dragon, *i.e.*, between order and anarchy, the life-giving spirit and dead matter

[1] *Paradise Lost*, ii. 891-897, and 910-914.

[2] Boscawen, *Bible and the Monuments*, 87 ; B. Museum, *Handb of Assyr. Antiq.*, 44.

[3] So Icel. *Gap*, Chaos (the Gaper).

developed into a moral dualism between light and darkness, right and wrong, God and Satan. To the ancient Babylonians the origin of evil was " the loud misrule of Chaos" out of which this beautiful world of Order was drawn by the superior might of the Creator. And so Tiâmat, at first the personification of anarchy, became the ideal antipathy of all that is good and fair, and eventually the leader of the powers of darkness, the Evil Spirit. In one incantation, *e.g.*, a Babylonian beseeches his god to "destroy Tiâmat, strike the unpitying evil one." [1] It was an old Accadian belief that the human race, originally innocent, was seduced by the temptations of the dragon of the deep; [2] just as in the sacred books of the Parsis the fiendish serpent, as agent of Augra Mainyu (Ahriman), the evil principle, strives to destroy or mar the world of the good Creator. [3]

[1] Sayce, *Hib. Lect.*, 384. In the Gnostic speculations of the Ophites, Demiurgus, the creator of the material world, was filled with rage and envy at the superiority of man to himself, and his evil aspect was reflected in the abyss as in a mirror; this becoming animated, came forth as Satan, the serpent formed (*Ophiomorphos*) the embodiment of envy and cunning (C. R. King, *The Gnostics*, 29). By this dragon-formed ruler of the world the evil soul is seized and swallowed up on its departure from the body (Ib. 128). The Naaseni, another Gnostic sect, held that the serpent, Naas (Heb. *Náchásh*), was the watery principle from which all things proceed (Hippolytus, *Refut. of All Heresies*, bk. v. ch. 4).

[2] Sayce, *Bab. Literature*, 46.

[3] *Zend-Avesta* (ed. Darmesteter), i. lxiii. This, too, was a water-serpent (i. 5).

This Dragon, of misshapen body and malignant disposition, the enemy of all righteousness, was the prototype of the Hebrew Satan. "The Babylonian devil," says Dr. Budge, "is not much to be distinguished from the Satan "[1] we read of in the Bible. "It is difficult," says Professor Sayce, "not to trace in the lineaments of Tiâmat the earliest portraiture of the mediæval devil."[2] "When the Semitic faith existed in its full purity, Satan, the adversary, was but an angel and minister of the Lord [e.g., Job i.], and the Supreme God was the Creator alike of good and evil, of light and darkness " [Isa. xlv. 7].

"The Empire of Chaos was really a stranger to genuine Semitic belief; it was a legacy left by the Accadians, which was assimilated and adapted by the Semites as best they could."[3] Tiâmat, the aboriginal Deep, is often referred to as the mother of a brood of composite monsters, half-beast, half-bird, the rudimentary creatures of a previous æon, corresponding to the saurians and amphibious reptiles of an extinct

---

[1] *Babylonian Life and Hist.*, 138.

[2] *Hib. Lect.*, 102 ; *cf.* 283. It is noteworthy that by the parallelism of Ps. lxxxix. 9, 10, the proud sea and Rahabh ("The Noisy" storm-dragon or sea-serpent, not = Egypt) are declared to be the *enemies* of Jahveh, which He routs with His mighty arm ; see Goldziher, p. 42. It was "in the days of old, the generations of ancient times" [*i.e.*, the creation] that Jahveh "cut Rahabh in pieces and pierced the dragon " (Isa. li. 9). There is an interesting transition in v. 10 from the legendary to the historical.

[3] *Hib. Lect.*, 346.

world.[1]   " Warriors with the bodies of birds of the
desert, men with the faces of ravens, Tiâmat gave
them suck," says an Accadian tablet.[2]   These too
were routed by the sun-god Merodach.   The disappearance of these " dragons of the prime that tare
each other in their slime " was a part of the victory
of light over darkness, of the heavenly powers over
the Titanic monsters of Chaos.

The German theologian Lange, though necessarily
unacquainted with the late Babylonian discoveries,
came to the conclusion on other grounds that Satan
was originally the chief and centre of the primeval
world, in which colossal serpents, lizards and other
monstrous amphibia predominated ; and for this
reason, he thinks, after its destruction he was
designated as the Dragon.   He is a survival, " the
ethical giant-fossil from the age of the pre-human
earth-formation.   But though that demon-earth has
been judged and set aside by the formation of the

---

[1] Palæontology knows of a winged and feathered creature,
the pterodactyl, between bird and reptile, with lizard-like head
and teeth and tail, and birdlike pinions, feet and breast
(G. Allen, *Darwin*, 167), which recalls Tiâmat.   S. Augustin held
these monsters to be no part of God's good creation.   The
fossil skeleton of a saurian was once shown at Aix as that of a
legendary dragon (*Dict. Christ. Antiq.*, s. v. Dragon).   See also
H. N. Hutchinson, *Extinct Monsters*, 61, 121 ; F. P. Cobbe, *False
Beasts and True*, 75-79 ; Spenser, *Faërie Queene*, II. 12, xxii.-xxv.
Mr. A. H. Keene conjectures that the original of the dragon was
some huge crocodile infesting the Euphrates, which primitive
man encountered (Bousset, *Anti-Christ Legend*, prol. xix.).

[2] *Records of the Past*, xi. 109.

human earth, yet as smothered Chaos it has in
various ways an influence on the tone of the present
world's history. From time to time the tones of
that insular antiquity break forth. The billows
[= Tiâmat] again roar, and mingle sea and land, and
miasmata are exhaled from the swamps." ¹

Berôssus, in his later account, says that in the
primeval darkness and abyss of waters there
existed monstrous animals of composite form
presided over by Thamti (Tiâmat), which being
unable to bear the light of the sun were extermi-
nated by Bel (Merodach). A reminiscence of these
creatures, he adds, survived in the winged bulls and
cherubic figures of the monuments and in idols, like
Dagon, of different animal forms combined.² These
monsters, it seems, in the new creation were
banished to the depths of ocean, the domain of
Tiâmat, where in Bible times they still existed.
In opposition, however, to the Babylonian belief
these *tannînîm* or sea-monsters are expressly claimed
by the author of Genesis as a part of Jehovah's
creation: "Elôhîm created the great sea-monsters"

¹ *Life of Christ*, ii. 44. Poisons and other banes Lange con-
ceives to be also survivals from the abolished pre-Adamite
world. He would probably include here parasites, designed
apparently only to inhabit and afflict other animals, which the
Gnostics were fain to ascribe to Demiurgus, the bad Creator.
Byron curiously anticipated this idea of the pre-Adamite monsters existing as mighty phantoms in Hades in his *Cain* (act ii.
sc. 2), which is worth comparing.

² Sayce, *Hib. Lect.*, 369, 373, 393 ; Lenormant, *Chald. Magic*, 53

(i. 21). Their nursing-mother, Tiâmat, which is only obscurely referred to there (i. 2) in the mention of Tĕhôm, as if purposely kept in the background, came into greater prominence at a later period when more familiarity with Babylonian ideas prevailed among the Jews. In the apocryphal book of Bel and the Dragon we recognise Tiâmat at once in the Dragon of Babylon with which Daniel had so curious an encounter. "In that same place there was a great Dragon which they of Babylon worshipped" (v. 23). Daniel, refusing to join in its worship, undertakes to slay it without sword or staff. He achieves his object by taking pitch, fat, and hair, "which he did seethe together and make lumps thereof; this he put in the Dragon's mouth, and so the Dragon burst in sunder; and Daniel said, Lo, these are the gods ye worship" (v. 27). Not only is this serpent-god of the Babylonians an undoubted survival of the ancient Tiâmat, but in Daniel's mode of destroying it by thrusting combustibles down its open throat there is an evident reminiscence of Merodach's (Bel's) treatment of his draconic antagonist when he burst her open by forcing storm and thunderbolts[1] through her

---

[1] In the Aramaic original of Theodotion's additions to the Book of Daniel the thunderbolts have become "iron hatchets" around which the bolus of flax, &c. is wrapped; the Dragon swallowing this, is killed by "the points (or spurs) of the hatchets" (Dr. Gaster, *Proc. Soc. Bib. Archœology*, xvii. pp. 86 and 92).

gaping jaws.[1]   This apocryphal story, as Mr. Ball
observes, existed in Aramaic and Hebrew at a very
early date.   It may have been evolved, he suggests,
out of the words of Jeremiah : " He hath swallowed
me up like a dragon, he hath filled his belly,"
spoken originally of the King of Babylon (l. 34).
Both passages, however, are ultimately founded on
the old legend of Merodach and Tiâmat, with which
the Jews became acquainted at Babylon, as the
Talmud shows.[2]   We can see also that in the
canonical Book of Daniel the imagery of the vision
in the seventh chapter was suggested by Babylonian
·types, when the prophet saw the four winds breaking forth upon the great sea, and there coming
forth from it four great · beasts, one like a lion
with eagle's wings, another like a leopard with four
wings of a fowl (vv. 2–7).

In the Greek addition to the Book of Esther,
called " the Dream of Mordecai," Haman, as the
typical enemy of the Jews, is represented as a
dragon engaged in mortal conflict with Mardocheus

---

[1] A rabbinical writer, Josippon ben Gorion, says that Daniel
destroyed the dragon by fastening something like *iron combs*
together, back to back, baiting them with fat, pitch, and
sulphur, and casting the mass into its open mouth. " Instru-
menta ferrea instar pectinum . . . tergum conjungens tergo "·
(Selden, *Syntag.*, 2, *De Belo et Dracone*, cap. 17). This is an exact
description of the thunderbolts, as figured in the hand of
Merodach on the monuments when warring with Tiâmat, *e.g.*
on the Calah bas-relief in the Brit. Museum. Appendix B.

[2] C. J. Ball, *The Apocrypha, Speaker's Comm.*, ii. 345, 348.

(Mordecai), as the champion of the righteous people, whose name is only a Hebraised form of Merodach,[1] the light-god; but, though an aberration from the primitive story, the latter also takes the form of a dragon, or perhaps of one of the winged dævas of the Persians. Some echoes of the original are perceivable in the circumstance that Mardocheus' victory is declared to be the victory of light and the sunrise on " a day of darkness and obscurity;" while "a great flood, even much water," is an incident of the struggle. " There was light and the sun and much water."[2]   It is the war of the religion of Israel against the religion of Heathenism, elsewhere exhibited in Michael withstanding the Prince of the Kingdom of Persia (Dan. x. 13).[3]   The passage is as follows: " Behold, two great dragons came forth ready to fight, and their cry was great. And at their cry all nations were prepared to battle that they might fight against the righteous people. And, lo, a day of darkness and obscurity, tribulation and anguish, affliction and great uproar, upon earth. . . . Upon their cry as it were from a little fountain was

---

[1] Sayce, *Ezra and Nehemiah*, 101. "The two dragons are I and Aman " (Esther x. 7 (Lxx.)).

[2] Ibid., x. 6. The Midrash Esther says that the dragons were *tannînîm*, sea-monsters (Cassell, *Esther*, p. xx.), and that Haman cried, 'As great fishes swallow little fishes, so will I swallow Israel " (*Speaker's Comm.*, *Apocrypha*, i. 373).

[3] *Cf.* Michael and the Dragon, Rev. xii.   Haman conceived as a dragon was to be assailed by the Messiah (Cassell, xxiv.).

made a great flood, even much water. The light
and the sun rose up, and the lowly were exalted, and
devoured the glorious."[1]

6. **Dragons of the Bible.**—If Tiâmat lurks
perdu in the Hebrew conception of the great deep
of Genesis i. 2, we might fairly expect that it would
sometimes emerge into consciousness in the later
literature of that people ; and so we find it does.
It is an interesting study to trace the survival of
this semi-mythological personification of the Deep
as a dragon in the various books of the Bible.[2]
Its curious persistence proves how strong an impression the Babylonian legend had made on the
Hebrew mind. Professor Gunkel has drawn attention to the subject in a very ingenious and suggestive book,[3] and Professor Cheyne has given a
general acceptance to his conclusions.[4] Let us
glance at some of the references which they supply.
In Ezekiel Pharaoh is compared to "the great
dragon (*tannîm*) that lieth in the midst of his
rivers" (xxix. 3), and again, "Thou art as a dragon
in the seas" (xxxii. 2). Isaiah says: "In that day

---

[1] Esther (Lxx.) xi. 6–11. Gr. text B for " the lowly," &c.
has " the rivers were swollen."

[2] Hengstenberg on Ps. lxxiv. 13, 14. *Cf.* in an English poet :
  "The sea-beast he tosseth his foaming mane ;
  He bellows aloud to the misty sky."
          (B. Cornwall, *Eng. Songs,* 1844, p. 128.)

[3] H. Gunkel, *Schöpfung und Chaos in Urzeit und Endzeit,* 1895,
see esp. pp. 69–81.

[4] *Critical Review,* July 1895, pp. 256-266.

Jahveh will punish leviathan, the winding serpent, and He shall slay the dragon (*tannîn*) that is in the sea" (xxvii. 1). And similarly the Psalmist: "Thou brakest the heads of the dragons (*tannînîm*, the sea-monsters) in the waters" (lxxiv. 13).[1] This sea-dragon is frequently referred to under the title of Râhâb, "The Violent," or "The Raging One," and always with something of the same mythological significance. It is the Assyrian *rahâbu*, a sea-monster,[2] and sometimes it is identified with the crocodile of Egypt. Thus Job says:

"He stirreth up the sea with His power,
And by His understanding He smiteth through Rahab ['the Dragon' (Renan)].[3] . . .
His hand hath pierced the gliding serpent" (xxvi. 12, 13).

---

[1] All the learning of the ancients on the subject of dragons will be found in Bochart, *Opera*, 1692, ii. colls. 428-440; Aldrovandus, *Monstrorum Historia*, 1642; Topsell, *Historie of Serpents*, 1608, 153-173; Fergusson, *Tree and Serpent Worship; Sir Tristrem*, ed. Scott, 90-94, 309-312; Hershon, *Treasures of Talmud*, 308; Scott, *The Pirate*, note D; Didron, *Christian Iconography*, ii. 115, 259; Chambers, *Book of Days*, i. 540; Sébillot, *Légendes, Croyances et Superstitions de la Mer*, 1886; F. S. Basset, *Legends and Superstitions of the Sea*, 1885; Spenser, *F. Queene*, I. vii. 16-18, 31, 44, and xi. *passim*; E. Goldsmid, *Un-natural History, Myths of Ancient Science*, iii. 18 *seq*. The "dragon-well" of Neh. ii. 13, seems to point to some Jewish folk-lore connected with a water-spring. *Cf. Percy Folio MS.*, i. 468, ll. 1484 *seq*. Some Highland sea lochs are believed to be haunted by a dragon (Campbell, *Tales of W. Highlands*, iv. 338). *Cf.* the legendary serpents of the Norwegian lakes, Mjösen, Snaasen, &c. (A. Faye, *Norske Folke-sagn*).

[2] Sayce, *Hib. Lect.*, 258.

[3] Delitzsch understands it to be the dragon in the heavens which by winding round the sun causes it to be eclipsed.

And again : " The helpers of Rahab (the rebellious
sea-monster) stoop under Him " (ix. 13), with which
we may compare a difficult passage in the Psalms :
" Blessed is the man . . . that looketh not to the
Rahabs [*Rehâbîm*], and to lying apostates " (Ps. xl.4).[1]
In Isaiah we find Rahab, *tannîn*, and *tĕhôm* brought
_together in one verse : " Art thou not it that cut
Rahab in pieces, that pierced the dragon (*tannîn*),
art not thou it which dried up the waters of the
great deep (*tĕhôm*) ? (li. 9). A passage earlier than
these in the prophecy of Amos makes mention of a
huge serpent at the bottom of the sea[2] ready to
devour God's enemies : " Though they hide themselves from my sight in the bottom of the sea,
thence will I command the serpent and he shall
bite them " (ix. 3). It is a widespread belief. The
Mussulmans have a tradition that the *tannîn* or
waterspout lives in the depths of the sea from
which it comes up at times in the form of a black
serpent.[3] Robertson Smith holds that the Leviathan (Livyâthân, the " twisting " monster) was likewise a personification of the water-spout.[4] Behemoth, as well as Rahab and Leviathan, is probably

---

[1] Gunkel, p. 40; see *Crit. Rev.*, v. 265. Rahab is the Assyrian
rahâbu, a sea-beast, and has been identified with the dragon
Tiâmat (Sayce, *Hib. Lect.*, 258).

[2] Japanese folk-lore tells of a huge four-footed serpent dwelling
at the bottom of the sea.

[3] Sébillot, *Légendes de la Mer*, ii. 119.

[4] *Religion of the Semites*, 1889, 161. *Cf.* " Dragons and all
deeps " (Ps. cxlviii. 7). Kuenen thinks that Levi (" the twister,
akin to Leviathan) was originally the mythic serpent or dragon
which fights against the sun, from which the tribe took its

only another phase of the same monster of the deep, the chaos-dragon, which the Creator subdued in the world's infancy, and banished to the profundity of the ocean.[1] It is difficult not to see here also the germ of the sea-serpent legend, which has exhibited such wonderful vitality till this day.[2] Whether the Chinese dragon Lung ("that which ascends") is also a descendant of Tiāmat is more doubtful, though the prehistoric connection between the Chinese and the Accadians, which M. de la Couperie and Mr. Ball have traced, at least renders it possible. Hiding in the depths all the winter it mounts into the sky at the vernal equinox, and from the radical idea of "rising" which belongs to it, and so of loftiness and pre-eminence, it has become the well-known symbol of imperial power which plays such an important part in Chinese ceremonial.[3]

name (*Nat. and Universal Religions*, 316). *Cf.* the Serpentine god, Anyi-ewo (A. B. Ellis, *Ewe-speaking Peoples of Slave Coast*, 47, 48,.

[1] Gunkel and Cheyne, *Crit. Rev.*, v. 262.

[2] Compare the Assyrian "great beasts of the sea" (*tiamtu =* Tiāmat) (Boscawen, *Bible and the Monuments*, 71) ; Buddhist cosmology tells of a great fish in the middle of the sea which is 9000 miles long (Du Bose, *The Dragon, Image, and Demon*, 210). For the sea-serpent, reference may be made to Pontoppidan, *Nat. Hist. of Norway* (1751), ii. 210; C. Gould, *Mythical Monsters*, 1888; E. Goldsmidt, *Un-natural History of Myths of Ancient Science*, 1886; T. Hawkins, *Book of the Great Sea Dragons*; F. E. Hulme, *Myth-Land*, 1886; R. A. Proctor, *Nature Studies*, 1894; H. Lee, *Sea Monsters Unmasked*, 52-103; Mangin, *Mysteries of the Sea*, 303 *seq.*; Basset, *Legends of the Sea*, 219 *seq.*

[3] J. Edkins, *Study of Chinese Characters*, 39, 135. *Cf.* Welsh

7. **The Sea a Rebellious Power.**—Though the Hebrews probably did not always remember that the monstrous Tiâmat (Tĕhôm) was itself nothing else but the dangerous primeval flood which Jahveh had to subjugate and set limits to before the orderly work of creation could proceed, still down to the latest times they retained a conscious feeling that this vanquished deep was a hostile and refractory power which was held in constant restraint by the might of the Omnipotent, and needed to be watched continually lest it should break out in rebellion and bring back the primeval Chaos—" Chaos innumeros avidum confundere mundos."[1]

This is the meaning of Job's complaint, " Am I a sea (*yâm*) or a sea-monster (*tannin*), that thou settest a watch over me ?" (vii. 12), where the reference in *yâm* is to the " heaven-assaulting sea, the tumultuous primitive abyss, which God watched and confined, and still watches and enchains, lest it overwhelm the world, and in *tannîn* to those vast creatures with which the early waters of creation teemed " (Gen. i. 21).[2] Similarly in other passages, " Who shut up

Pendragon. So the great Egyptian dragon Apepi (= " the storm cloud ") means "he who mounts up" (Renouf, *Trans. Soc. Bib. Archæology*, viii. pt. 2).

[1] Lucan, *Phars.*, vi. 696. So Michelet, addressing the waves as foaming beasts : "Monstres, que voulez-vous donc ? N'êtes-vous pas soûls des naufrages ? Que demandez-vous ? La mort universelle, la suppression de la terre et le retour au Chaos ! " (*La Mer*). " The seas encroaching crueltie " (Spenser).

[2] A. B. Davidson, *Comm. in loco.*

the sea with doors," asks Jahveh, " when I . . . .
prescribed for it my decree, And set bars and doors,
And said, 'Hitherto shalt thou come, but no further; And here shall thy proud waves be stayed?"
(xxxviii. 8–11). Again, "Thou hast set them a
bound that they may not pass over, that they turn
not again to cover the earth " (Ps. civ. 9). With
this should be compared an ancient Babylonian
tablet which says of the conqueror of Tiâmat, *i.e.*,
the Creator :

" Merodach a wide space on the face of the Deep
bound round; He made dust, and poured it on the
space. . . . The Lord Merodach around the sea made
an embankment;"[1] and the words of Solomon in the
eighth chapter of Proverbs :

" Before the hills were brought forth . . .
Or the highest part of the dust of the world . . .
When He set a circle upon the face of the depth . . .
When He strengthened the fountains of the Deep,
When He gave to the sea His decree,
That the waters should not pass His commandment."

(vv. 25–29.)

Passages like these imply that the sea, like a wicked
rebel, if Jahveh were to remove his curbing hand,
would soon overflow the earth again and bring back
the confusion of Chaos (Tĕhôm).[2]   The subjugation

---

[1] Boscawen, *Bible and the Monuments*, 78, 81.   *Cf.*:

" I have seen
The ambitious ocean swell and rage and foam,
To be exalted with the threatening clouds."

(Shakspeare, *Julius Cæsar*, i. 3, 8.)

[2] A Spanish folk-tale tells how the sea, having broken through

of this turbulent creature is frequently appealed to as a proof of His Divine Omnipotence and determination to punish every other hostile and resisting power. Thus, in Jeremiah God demands of His revolting people, "Will ye not tremble at My presence, which have placed the sand for the bound of the sea, by a perpetual decree, that it cannot pass it? And though the waves thereof toss themselves, yet they cannot prevail; though they roar, yet they cannot pass over it" (v. 22).[1] The raging Deep is here the symbol of impotent hostility; and in the Apocalyptic books it is out of it that the monstrous powers of Antichrist are seen to arise.

In the Book of Jonah the sea appears as an angry being only to be appeased by the surrender of a victim. The engulfing sea-monster is only a more concrete form of the same conception, and on early Christian monuments it is often depicted as a dragon.[2]

The superstitious dread of the dangerous primeval ocean embodied in the Babylonian Tiâmat, with claw and fangs to typify its cruel savage náture and wings to indicate its mounting impetuosity, survived among the Semites in a fear and awe of the sea down to the latest times. As "the Great Green One" was at all

---

the limits set it by the Creator, which it had promised to obey, was punished for its disobedience (Sébillot, *Légendes de la Mer*, i. 6).

[1] *Cf.* Ex. xv. 8; Ps. lxv. 7; Isa. xvii. 12–14; li. 15; lix. 19.

[2] *Dict. of Christ. Antiq.*, s. v. Dragon; H. Lee, *Sea Monsters Unmasked*, 55; Goldziher, 28, 102.

times an object of dread to the ancient Egyptians,[1] as to the ancient Greek "there was nothing more evil than the sea to confound even the strongest man,"[2] so the Hebrews could never conquer a secret horror of that element, whose unfathomed depths for them reached down to the very gates of the lower world (Jonah ii. 6, 7).[3] Among most primitive peoples dislike and fear are the "sentiments inspired by the boundless insatiable ocean, which raves against its bounds like a beast of prey. In Aryan tongues its synonyms are the 'desert' and 'night.' It produces an impression of immensity, infinity, formlessness and barren changeableness, well suited to a notion of chaos" :[4]

> "The awful, pitiless sea,
> With all its terror and mystery,
> The dim, dark sea, so like unto death,
> That divides, and yet unites, mankind."[5]

---

[1] A. Erman, *Life in Ancient Egypt*, 15. They regarded the sea as impure and under the dominion of the spirit of evil, Set or Typhon. The "determinative" expressive of evil is added to *ûāt-oer*, "great water," the Egyptian word for the sea.

[2] Homer, *Odys.*, viii. 138. Compare the Hindu's dread of "the dark water," and Icel. Œgir, "the Awful One" = the sea (Grimm, *Teut. Myth.*, 237). See F. S. Bassett, *Legends of the Sea*, 12. Jensen observes that the Babylonians, unlike the Phœnicians, distrusted and feared the sea as an unexplored region given up to spectres and the dead. In the Gistubar Epic it is called "the water of the dead" (*Kosmologie der Babylonier*, 213).

[3] Kalisch, *Comm. on Jonah*, 137.

[4] D. G. Brinton, *Myths of the New World*, 209.

[5] Longfellow, *The Golden Legend*. "Moi aussi, je regardais

Spenser also has expressed this ancient feeling of repugnance to the sea as a source of mysterious danger :

> "'So to the sea we came ; the sea, that is
> A world of waters heaped up on hie,
> Rolling like mountaines in wide wildernesse,
> Horrible, hideous, roaring with hoarse crie.'
>   'And is the sea (quoth Coridon) so fearfull ? '
> 'Fearfull much more (quoth he) than hart can fear :
> Thousand wyld beasts with deep mouthes gaping direfull
> Therin stil wait poore passengers to teare.
> Who life doth loath, and longs death to behold,
> Before he die, alreadie dead with feare,
> And yet would live with heart halfe stonie cold,
> Let him to sea, and he shall see it there.'"[1]

Wordsworth, sharing the same feeling, could not see a ship put forth to sea without experiencing

> "Of the old sea some reverential fear."[2]

That ancient awe noticed by Wordsworth for the sea and its tremendous secrets, as De Quincey truly observes, is a feeling that has not, no, nor ever will, become entirely obsolete. "No excess of nautical skill will ever perfectly disenchant the great abyss from its terrors."[3] We are not surprised, therefore,

insatiablement cette mer. Je la regardais avec haine" (Michelet, *La Mer*).

[1] *Colin Clouts come Home Again*, *Works*, Globe ed., p. 551.

[2] *Where lies the Land*. To the modern Greek "the wicked sea" is suggestive of gloomy images of despair (E. Martinengo-Cesaresco, *Study of Folk Songs*, 39).

[3] *Works*, iii. 304. *Cf.* Pliny, *Nat. Hist.*, proem to Bk. xxxii. ; Bassett, *Legends of the Sea*, 12 ; V. Hugo, *Travailleurs de la Mer*, *passim*.

to find that in the Hebrew Scriptures this element is
a frequent metaphor not only for dreary confusion,
and peril, but for misery and calamity (*cf.* Job xxii.
11 ; Ps. xlii. 7).   As representing the original chaotic
water it is a manifestation of the destructive energies
of evil upon earth.[1]   Reduced to order and confined
it had received a place among the good works of
God, and its embankment was nothing less than a
victory over a bad revolting power.[2]   But the waters
of the sea are a surviving remnant of that raging
abyss, Tiâmat, which in the beginning made earth a
desolation (*bohû*).   Thus, as a cosmic symbol of sin
and rebellion when the wickedness of man called for
exemplary punishment it was again let loose upon
the earth in the Deluge—Chaos returned as in the
aboriginal Deep (Tĕhôm) [3] of waste and desolation.[4]

---

[1] The Chinese believe that the great flood B.C. 3100 was
caused by the evil spirit, Kung-Kung (Prejevalsky, *Mongolia*, i.
272).

[2] Baumgarten, *Apostolic Hist.*, iii. 232-3.

[3] It is curious to find the mythopœic feeling still surviving in
medieval Europe, and turning a destructive inundation into a
ravaging dragon.   St. Romanus, who is said to have constructed
embankments to check the overflowing of the river at Rouen in
the seventh century, was afterwards reputed to have delivered
the city from a dragon.   This monster was known as Gargouille,
a reminiscence of which still survives in the wide-mouthed
" gargoils " of our churches (Chambers, *Book of Days*, i. 540).

[4] So Byron's angel on the approach of the Deluge :

"Quit this chaos-founded prison,
To which the elements again repair,
To turn it into what it was."

(*Heaven and Earth*, sc. 3.)

In the mystic sense of Scripture this turbulent element—

> "The great sea, puft up with proud disdaine,
> To swell above the measure of his guise,
> As threatening to devoure all that his powre despise"[1]—

is the restless wicked world (Isa. lvii. 20), into which the Apocalyptic Dragon is cast down announcing woe (Rev. xii. 12). It is the symbol of worldly pride and tumultuous rebellion, of confusion and anarchy (St. Luke xxi. 25 ; Rev. viii. 8, 9 ; xiii. 1 ; Ps. lxv. 7) ;[2] cf. "Thou rulest the *pride* of the sea" (Ps. lxxxix. 9). We are now in a position to understand the full mystic significance of the otherwise enigmatical statement with which the Book of Revelation closes, that this dark image of sin and disorder, which has marred the earth from its very foundation, will have no place in the renovated world. In the new heaven and the new earth, wherein dwelleth righteousness, there will be "NO MORE SEA" (Rev. xxii. 1).[3] Tiâmat in all its manifold phases— whether we call it Tĕhôm, the Dragon, the Serpent, Satan, Anarchy, Evil, Sin, or Death[4]—shall be

---

[1] Spenser, *F. Q.*, ii. 12, 21.

[2] Wordsworth on Rev. xxi. 1 ; Hengstenberg, *Rev.*, vol. ii. p. 312 ; Macmillan, *Bible Teachings in Nature*, 293 *seq.*

[3] Gunkel, p. 370. The discourse to the Greeks concerning Hades, attributed to Josephus, says that in the heavenly kingdom there will not be "any fearful roaring of the sea, forbidding the passengers to walk on it" (*Works*, trans. Whiston, 1865, p. 638).

[4] The dragon idea seems to lie in the background of St. Paul's conception of death as a destructive monster armed with a

finally cast out of God's universe, and the complete victory of the God of Light shall be for ever consummated. Thus the Cycle of Scripture comes full circle, and in manifestly designed harmony the solemn note sounded in its opening chapter dies away in the closing scene of the great Drama, re-echoed in a higher key. Across the ages of the world's history " Deep calleth unto Deep "—Tĕhôm to Tĕhôm (Ps. xlii. 7)—ere it disappears and sinks for ever into the eternal calm.

8. **The Watery Hades—Tartaros.**—Akin to Tiâmat, the watery waste, in the Babylonian mythology was Ea, "the Spirit of the Deep," [1] who eventually came to be identified with another divinity, of similar attributes, Mul-lil, the mighty lord of the ghost-world or Hades.[2] Ea, the encircling ocean-stream, "the water under the earth," was easily confused with the underworld beyond and beneath, to which it was believed to form the entrance. As *inferus* passed over into *infernus*, so the world of Ea became the realm of Hades. It was Mul-lil, " the Ghost-lord," who according to the tablets caused the waters of the flood to come up upon the earth and destroy mankind,[3] which shows how much he and

deadly sting (1 Cor. xv. 55), which is Hosea's figure of Hades (Lxx. xiii. 14.)   [1] *Zi-apsu* (Sayce, *Hib. Lect.*, 233).

[2] Sayce, *Hib. Lect.*, 145, 359.

[3] "May he exorcise the sea-monster of Chaos" is part of a prayer to Ea. The queen of the infernal region, Allat, "lady of the lower abyss," was sometimes known as Tamti, the primordial deep (Lenormant, *Chald. Magic,* 116).

Ea had in common. Both alike exercised control over the world of waters, both alike were lords of the monsters of the underworld, whether they be dragons and serpents as in the one case, or ghosts and demons as in the other. The ancient Accadians, like ourselves, associating the ideas of profundity and wisdom, as we have already seen, believed Ea, the god of the primordial deep, to be also the god of wisdom, and spoke of him as "tal-tal," "The Very Wise." His world of mystery is the world of un-discovered secrets. Now as tal-tal would readily take the form of *tar-tar* by the law which prevails in many languages that *l* and *r* are interchangeable, one would be tempted to conjecture (though the con-necting links cannot be traced), that the word passed over to the Greeks and became their Tartaros, a name for the infernal region which has never received a satisfactory explanation.[1] However that may be, it

[1] Other eschatological names among the Greeks have been traced to a Babylonian origin, such as Hades (1, the god of the nether world; 2, the nether world itself), Erebus and Acheron. See *Trans. Soc. Biblical Archæology*, ii. 188; iii. 125. Fick and Curtius can give no account of Tartaros. Its origin has been sought in the Sanskrit *tâla-tâla*, "the hell of hells," a reduplication of *tâla*, hell (Ragozin, *Vedic India*, 363). There is reason, however, to suspect that τάρταρος in Greek originally denoted the troubled sea, and so it may be a horrific reduplica-tion of the root *ter, tar*, to tremble, seen in ταρταρίζω, to tremble, Sansk. *tar-anta-s*, the sea, *tar-ala-s*, trembling, as well as in θάλασσα, the sea (for τδρασσα), akin to ταράσσω, to trouble or agitate; the sea, as Curtius observes, obtaining its name from its restless tossing motion (*Greek Etym.*, ii. 319). "There is sorrow upon the sea; it cannot be quiet" (Jer. xlix. 23).

is interesting to note that the Greek Hell, Tartaros, had originally much the same nature as Tal-tal, the Wise Sea-god or Deep. There is evidence that in the earliest times it was a watery realm, not a fiery. To reach the Babylonian Hades the waters of the great reservoir of ocean had to be crossed. When Istar descended to its portals the words she addressed to its porter are "Opener of the waters, open thy gate."[1]   Indeed, Proclus notes that the ancients generally conceived the ocean as separating the visible world from the kingdom of the dead or Hades, so that such as went to Hades must first pass the ocean;[2]

> "Nos manet Oceanus circumvagus : arva, beata
> Petamus arva divites et insulas."[3]

Similarly, in the Book of Enoch, Hades is seen to be by a great sea which is towards the west, "the place whither all the waters of the deep flow," "the mouth of the deep." "This is the prison of the angels, and here they are held to eternity."[4]   Even Scripture so far condescends to the popular ideas as

[1] *Descent,* l. 14; Sayce, *Hib. Lect.,* 221 ; Lenormant, *Beginnings of History,* 371.

[2] Lenormant, *Chald. Magic,* 169. In the Egyptian *Book of the Dead,* the soul has to cross the waters to Elysium. In the *Chants Populaires de la Bretagne* (ed. Villemarqué), the soul, before it arrives at the lower regions, must pass the sea, beyond which the mouths of the Abyss open (p. 156).

[3] Horace, *Epod.* xvi. 42 ; see Ussher, *Answer to a Jesuit* (ed. 1835), p. 324.

[4] *Book of Enoch* (ed. Schodde), 89, 92.

to regard the depths of the sea as the realm of the
dead.[1] And Tartaros, there is reason to believe,
originally denoted a dark watery abyss in the heart
of the sea.[2] Plutarch implies that it was so called
from its coldness, comparing the verb ταρταρίζω to
shiver from cold,[3] to which Milton seems to refer
when he says that the Creating Spirit in his action
on the abyss

> " Downward purged
> The black, *tartareous*, *cold*, infernal dregs,
> Adverse to life." [4]

Hesiod, in like manner, represents Poseidon, the sea-
god, as setting gates to Tartaros to confine the
Titans (*Theog.*, 732); hard by its entrance was
Hydra, the water-serpent. So, in the Septuagint
version of Job xli. 31, the sea-monster Leviathan is
associated with Tartaros: "He considers the Tartaros of the abyss his captive." The prophet in the
Book of Jonah, when swallowed by the sea-monster
and covered by the deep, seemed to himself as one
that had entered into Hades : [5]

---

[1] Stier, *Works of Jesus*, ii. 169. See the passages quoted
below, pp. 53, 54.

[2] S. R. Maitland, *False Worship*, 33, 37.

[3] Plutarch, *Opera*, ii. 943. The deadly chill of night was the
symbol of the Zoroastrian evil spirit, Angrô-Mainyûs (Perrot and
Chipiez, *Art in Persia*, 13). In the Northern Mythology the
realm of Hel was a region of cold and mist.

[4] *Paradise Lost*, vii. 237-9.

[5] See Kalisch, *in loco*. Prof. Cheyne suggests that the monster
which swallowed Jonah was Rahab, "the raging one," *i.e.*, the

"Out of the belly of Sheòl did I cry . . .
For Thou didst cast me into the depth, in the heart of the
    seas,
And the flood was around me . . .
The waters compassed me about, even to the soul,
The Deep (*Tĕhôm*) was round about me.
The weeds were wrapped about my head;
I went down to the bottom of the mountains ;
The earth with her bars (closed) upon me for ever."

(iii. 3-6.)

The last words here refer to the barriers which
were conceived as separating the earth from Sheòl
lying beneath the sea.[1] The eschatological figures
employed by Jonah rendered this passage particu-
larly appropriate for our Lord's purpose when He
wished to speak of His own resurrection from the
world of the dead : " So shall the Son of Man be
three days and three nights in the heart of the
earth " (Matt. xii. 40), where the subterranean abyss
of Sheòl is denoted by " the heart of the earth," as it
was by " the heart of the sea " in Jonah, and the
descent into Hades is referred to.[2] Several other
passages of the Old Testament point to the same

storm-dragon (*cf.* Isa. xxvii. 1; Jer. li. 44); *Theolog. Review,*
1887, p. 215. See above, p. 38. Compare
             " Some envious surge
Will in his brinish bowels swallow him."
            (Shakspere, *Tit. Andronicus,* iii. 1, 96.)

[1] The dismal region of Arali, the Babylonian Hades, was
called " the support of Chaos " (Ragozin, *Chaldæa,* 157).

[2] See Lange on St. Matt. xii. 22 ; Stier, *Words of Jesus,* ii. 169 ;
Maitland, *False Worship,* 50; and Faber's speculative book,
The Many Mansions in the House of the Father, 338 *seq.*

conclusion, that Sheôl, the dark abode of the dead, was conceived by the Jews as lying at the bottom of the deep. Thus Jahveh asks of Job:

> " Hast thou entered into the springs of the Sea?
> Or hast thou walked in the recesses of the Deep (Tĕhôm)?[1]
> Have the Gates of Death been revealed unto thee?
> Or hast thou seen the Gates of the Shadow of Death?"
>
> (Job xxxviii. 16, 17.)

Still plainer is the remarkable statement that the nether-world of the Shades or departed spirits (*Inferi*) lies at the bottom of the sea:

> " The Shades-of-the-dead (Rephâim [2]) tremble
> Beneath the waters, and the inhabitants thereof:
> Sheôl is naked before Him,
> And Abaddon [3] hath no covering " (Job xxvi. 5. 6).

The Psalmist also places Sheôl in the *tĕhôm* or deep:

> "Thou shalt bring me up again from the depths (*tĕhôm*) of the earth " (lxxi. 20).[4]

---

[1] " At the bottom of the abyss " (Renan).

[2] The Rephâim were the spirits or phantoms (vanæ imagines —Hor.) of the dead. They were supposed to be a Titanic race buried beneath the sea (Renan, *Hist. of Israel*, i. 191 and 109). See F. Böttcher, *De Inferis*, 1846, p. 94 *seq.*, and 161.

[3] We shall see presently that, in the Apocalypse, Abaddon (Destruction) was the angel of the abyss or deep of evil spirits. The Jinns of the Arabians come up out of the waters. All such subterranean beings are excluded from worship in the exhaustive threefold division of creatures in Exodus xx. 4.

[4] *Cf.* "Every knee should bend of heavenly, earthly and *subterranean* beings " (Phil. ii. 10). Hades lies in the interior of the earth according to Tertullian, *De Anima*, cap. 55; "the lower parts of the earth" (*Eph.* iv. 9). See Delitzsch, *Psychology*, 477; Brinton, *Essays of an Americanist*, 126.

S. Paul even holds similar language when he puts
the question, "Who shall descend into *the abyss?*
that is, to bring Christ up from the dead" (Rom.
x. 7). The meaning of "abyss" here is determined
by the passage in Deuteronomy (xxx. 13) which he
is citing, "Neither is it [the Word] beyond *the sea,*
that thou shouldest say, Who shall go over *the sea*
for us, and bring it unto us?" The other side of
the sea (τὸ πέραν τῆς θαλασσῆς—Lxx.) is equated
with the abyss, and both with the place of the dead.
This elucidates the meaning of the fine passage in
Psalm cxxxix.:

> "If I make my bed in *Sheôl,* behold Thou art *there.*
> If I raise the wings of the dawn,
> And settle down *at the extremity of the sea :*
> Even *there* shall Thy hand lead me" (8-10).

The parallelism shows that the meaning is that, even
in the region of the dead, which is situated at the
furthest verge of the ocean, God would be present
with him.

The Greeks entertained similar notions with
regard to their infernal regions. Homer represents
Hades, the King of the Shades, as in fear lest the
earth-shaking sea-god, Poseidon, should break down
into his realms: [1]

> "The infernal monarch, heard alarmed,
> And springing from his throne, cried out in fear

---

[1] *Iliad,* xx. 61-66. Poseidon was in Phœnician called Tân,
and is represented on coins as a deity with a fish's tail and
trident ; on the obverse are two *tannin* (sea-monsters) (Lenormant, *Beginnings of Hist.,* 530).

> Lest Neptune, breaking through the solid earth,
> To mortals and immortals should lay bare
> His dark and drear abode of gods abhorred." [1]

In the *Odyssey* (xi. 155–158) the shade of his
mother addresses Odysseus with the words:

> " How is it, O my son, that you alive,
> This deadly-darksome region underdlive ?
> 'Twixt which and earth so many mighty seas
> And horrid currents interpose their prease [throng],
> Oceanus in chief ? " [2]

With these references may be compared the titles
of the god of the Babylonian under-world, " King of
the water-deep " (*Sar apsi*) ; " King of the death-
flood," which encircles the nether-world ; " King of
the water-house " in the depth of ocean.[3]

9. **The Deep as Hell.**—We have seen how the
Babylonian conception of the unreclaimed watery
Chaos developed into an infernal power ; in one direction, as the Dragon Serpent, or Evil Spirit, and in
another direction into an infernal or lower region into
which the souls of men descend after death. As
Tiâmat cherished in her dark depths all monstrous

---

[1] Lord Derby, *Iliad*, xx. ll. 70–75.

[2] Chapman, i. p. 255 (Lib. Old Auth.). Compare Spenser :
> " Bold men, presuming life for gaine to sell,
> Dare tempt that gulf, and in those wandring stremes
> Seek waies unknowne, waies leading down to hell."

(*Colin Clouts come Home Again*, *Works*, 551, Globe ed.)
Delitzch equates the Hebrew Sheôl ("The Hollow "), Hades,
with the Egyptian *tian*, the deep, the subterranean world (*New
Comm. on Genesis*, ii. 264). Compare Domdaniel, *infra*.

[3] A. Jeremias, *Vorstellungen vom Leben nach dem Tode*, p. 67.

forms of evil, so among the Hebrews the great Deep
was the abode of Rahab, the storm-dragon, which
was only another form of Tiâmat, and in later times
interpreted to be Satan.   Thus Job, speaking of the
Almighty, says :

" He stilleth the sea with His power,
  And by His understanding He smiteth through Rahab . . .
  His hand hath pierced the gliding serpent " (xxvi. 12, 13).

Here the Septuagint translates the last line, " By
His command He hath destroyed the Apostate
Dragon," [1] and Origen, commenting on the passage,
says it is certain that by the Apostate (or fugitive)
Dragon is to be understood the Devil himself,[2] who
is essentially of a cold nature.   " In the sea also,"
he adds, "the dragon is said to reign.   For the
prophet intimates that the serpent and dragon,
which certainly is referred to one of the wicked
spirits, is also in the sea [alluding probably to
Ezek. xxxii. 2, "Thou art as a dragon in the
seas"].   And elsewhere the prophet says, "I will

[1] The apocryphal " Acts of Thomas " (32) mentions " the dragon
inhabiting the abyss of Tartarus " (Grimm, *New Test. Dict.*, s. v.
Abyss).   So Leviathan (Job iii. 8) is the chaos-dragon which
lies in a charmed sleep in the hushed ocean (Cheyne).   Compare
" Rebuke thou the beast of the reeds " (Ps. lxviii. 31), *i.e.*, Behemoth, the chaos-monster ; and Typhon, the dragon overwhelmed
by Zeus' thunderbolts, one with the Phœnician Tzephôn, struck
down beneath the waters of the sea of reeds (Lenormant,
Beginnings of History, 551 *seq.*).

[2] Origen, *De Principiis*, bk. i. ch. 5, *sub fin.* ; Warburton, *Div.
Leg.*, iii. 118 (ed. Tegg).

draw out my holy sword upon the dragon, the flying serpent, upon the dragon the crooked serpent, and will slay him" (Isa. xxvii. 1). And again he says, " Even though they hide from my eyes and descend into the depths of the sea, there will I command the serpent and it shall bite them " (Amos ix. 3). In the Book of Job also he is said to be the " king of all things in the waters " (xli. 34).[1] "The dragon who is in the sea" (Isa. xxvii.' 1) was similarly understood by S. Jerome to be the Devil.[2] In medieval Latin, as De Gubernatis notes in his chapter on " the Serpent and the Aquatic Monster," Hydros or " water-serpent " was a name of the devil, who was also sometimes identified with Neptunus under the name of Aquatiquus or god of the waters. He adds that a demon called *Dracus* (from *draco*) was believed to haunt streams, and that generally the serpent-devil appears in special connection with the infernal waters.[3] This marine character of the Evil One is widely traceable in folk-lore. There is an Arabic

[1] Origen, *De Principiis*, ii. 8 (i. 123, Ante-Nic. Lib.). *R. V.* " He (Leviathan) is King over all the sons of pride."

[2] *Comm. in loco.* Old English writers very commonly speak of Satan as the dragon, owing to the apocalyptic use of the term mentioned below (*cf.* Ps. xci. 13 ; Grimm, *Teut. Myth.*, 998).

.." Done is a battell on the dragon blak,
    Our campioun Christ confoundit has his force."
                    (Dunbar, *Anct. Scot. Poems*, 1770, p. 85.)

" The old dragon under ground . . .
    Swindges the scaly horrour of his folded tail."
                    (Milton, *Hymn on Nativity*, l. 172.)

[3] *Zoological Mythology*, ii. 390–1. See Du Cange, *s. v.* Dracus.

superstition, *e.g.*, that the huge hand of Satan may be seen rising out of the ocean to seize any one who ventures to sail on the sea of darkness (*Mare Tenebrosum*, the Atlantic).[1] An Irish eighth century life of St. Fechin ascribes the savagery of a swelling tempestuous sea to "Satan himself assisting from beneath."[2]

In the Babylonian mythology the abyss of waters was also the appointed abode of demons and the place of their punishment. There the seven evil spirits have their dwelling, who, along with Tiâmat— *i.e.*, the storm-winds in conjunction with the Deep— conspire to tear down the heavens and throw nature into its primitive anarchy.[3] They are frequently mentioned in the tablets—*e.g.*:

"Those seven, the evil gods, the serpents of death, who have no fear,
Those seven, the evil gods, who swoop like the deluge,
Swoop upon the world like a storm."[4]

In the great mother-deep Bahu (= *Bohu*, "the

---

[1] Bassett, *Legends of the Sea*, 14.

[2] *Nineteenth Century*, No. 217, p. 422. Nothing seems known of "the mysteries of the dragon," which formed a part of the Eleusinian rite (Clem. Alex., *Exhort. to Heathen*, ch. ii.). "Old Nick," a name for the devil in folk-speech, was' originally O. Eng. *Nicor*, a sea-monster or water-demon (Icel. *nikr*) ; Beowulf "on the waves slew the nickers by night" (l. 422) ; "sea-dragons and nickers" (l. 1427). The devil is called *Celidrus* (= χέλυδρος, water-serpent) in a medieval writer (Grimm, *Teut. Myth.*, 1604).

[3] G. Smith, *Chaldean Account of Genesis* (ed. Sayce), 114.

[4] Sayce, *Hib. Lect.*, 465.

waste "), who was also "the lady of the house of death," these demons were assigned their home.[1] Another name by which they were known was Annúna-ge, or "Masters of the underworld,"[2] and in this capacity they were the agents of the infernal goddess Allat, "the lady of the gloomy pit"; in fact, virtually devils. It was these Annúna-ge, or lords of the subterranean water, who brought the flood over the earth, according to the Deluge tablets.[3] Another inscription says :

> " In the abyss of the deep seven are they.
> Pity and kindness know they not . . .
> Evil are they, baleful are they." [4]

When they issue forth upon the earth it is in the guise of pestilent and destructive winds, and their representations on the monuments wear forms of the most repulsive hideousness, which strongly resemble the devils of the medieval illuminators.[5] If Tiâmat is the prototype of Satan himself, the Annúna-ge of

---

[1] Sayce, *Hib. Lect.*, 262–3. An account of their rebellion and downfall is given in the tablets (*Records of the Past*, v. 163 ; vii. 127).

[2] They were opposed to the Igigi or spirits of the upper air (angels) (Jeremias, *Babylonisch-Assyrischen Vorstell. nach dem Tode*, 72 ; Sayce, *Hib. Lect.*, 183 ; Lenormant, *Chald. Magic*, 164, 17, 27).

[3] Schrader, *Cuneiform Insc. and the Old Test.*, i. 57 ; Sayce, *Fresh Light from the Anct. Monuments*, 36.

[4] Maspero, *Hist. Ancienne*, 262–3. Orientals generally still believe that the sea is the dwelling-place of many of their spiritual enemies (Roberts, *Orient. Illustrations*, 27).

[5] Maspero, *Hist. Ancienne*, 256.

the deep are certainly the counterparts of the
demons. These, too, were commonly believed to be
busy in storms.[1] When Ferdinand, in *The Tempest*,
leaped into the sea, he cried, "Hell is empty, and
all the devils are here" (i. 2, 212). The eighth
century life of St. Fechin mentions that he could
not behold the sea in a great gale "without thinking
upon those evil powers and influences whose fury is
seen in that watery fury and their hellish hate and
turbulence in the beating of the sea against the
rocks, and the gnashing and twisting of their lost
and evil souls in the gnashing and twisting of the
froth."[2] In reading this graphic description we can
hardly help thinking of an incident in the tempest
on the sea of Galilee, when the Lord rebuked the
sea and the winds as if sentient creatures. We
may conjecture, perhaps, without irreverence, that
He was condescending to the modes of thought of
the terrified fishermen when He addressed each
raging element in turn with a direct personal word
of command: to the roaring wind, "Be silent!"
(σιώπα)—to the yawning deep, "Close thy mouth!"[3]

---

[1] Aubrey, *Miscellanies*. 1696, p. 141 (Lib. Old Auth.); Grimm,
Teut. Myth., 1000, 1015; Boswell, *Life of Johnson*, p. 277 (ed.
1876).

[2] *Nineteenth Century*, No. 217, p. 422.

[3] S. Mark iv. 39, πεφίμωσο, "Be muzzled!" Compare
"'Silence, ye troubled waves, and thou Deep, peace,'
Said then the Omnific Word; 'your discord end!'
And 'Chaos heard His voice.'"
(Milton, *Paradise Lost* vii. 216–221.)

The latter words recall the primitive idea of the
sea as a devouring open-mouthed monster,[1] ready to
swallow up the little bark which it had been cruelly
" tormenting."[2]

> " His deepe devouring jawes
> Wide gaped, liked the griesly mouth of hell,
> Through which into his darke abysse all ravin fell." [3]

The conscious being to whom the rebuke was
given, as the ultimate and moving cause of the
lawless state of the elements, no doubt was Satan,
" the author of all disorders alike in the natural and
spiritual world," which, indeed, was, as we have seen,
the primary conception of that " Anarch Old." In
like manner the walking of Jesus upon the stormy
billows (Matt. xiv. 24, 25) was very probably not
merely a thaumaturgic act to exhibit His mastery
over the tumultuous power of the deep, and so

---

[1] *Cf.*
> "Though every drop of water . . .
> Gape at widest to glut him."
>> (Shakspere, *Tempest*, i. 1. 63.)
> " Have I not heard the sea puff'd up with winds
> Rage like an angry boar ? "
>> (*Taming of the Shrew*, i. 2, 203.)

[2] S. Matthew, in his account of the other storm at sea, says
that the boat was "tormented ($\beta\alpha\sigma\alpha\nu\iota\zeta\dot{o}\mu\epsilon\nu o\nu$) by the waves "
(xiv. 24).   The personification suggested is, perhaps, also trace-
able in " the great shaking ($\sigma\epsilon\iota\sigma\mu\dot{o}s$) in the sea" of S. Matthew
(viii. 24), recalling the "earth-shaking" ('$E\nu o\sigma\dot{\iota}\chi\theta\omega\nu$), Poseidon
of Homer.

[3] Spenser, *F. Q.*, I. xi. 12.   So in the Zend-Avesta storms and
other convulsions of nature are caused by the Evil One, Angra
Mainyu (i. lvi. *seq.*).

His oneness with Him whose way is in the sea
(Ps. lxxvii. 19), who alone treadeth upon the waves
of the sea (Job ix. 8), but a parabolic action as
treading down the rebellious uprising of sin, disorder
and death,[1] and trampling on

> "The watery kingdom, whose ambitious head
> Spits in the face of heaven,"[2]

on the part of Him under Whose feet the head of
the serpent (Gen. iii. 15) and all His enemies
(1 Cor. xv. 25) are to be placed.

10. **Punishment of the Rebel Host.**—There
are distinct traces of a belief among the Babylonians
that a certain portion of the host of heaven revolted
against the Supreme God, and were in consequence
imprisoned in a gloomy region, an abode of desolation, in company with the vanquished monsters of
Tiâmat, primordial Chaos, on whose side they had
ranged themselves, just as in the Greek myth the
Titans, who along with Kronos had revolted against
Zeus, were confined in Tartaros.[3]   The "Descent of
Ishtar" says :

> "In Hades dwell the princes and nobles, [4]
> There dwell the monsters of the abyss,
> There dwelleth Etana" [called Titan by Berôssos].[5]

---

[1] Eusebius, *Dem. Evang.*, ix. 12.

[2] Shakspere, *Merch. of Ven.*, ii. 7, 45.

[3] Lenormant, *Beginnings of History*, 369–370 ; Æschylus,
Prom. Vinct., 227 ; Hesiod, *Theog.*, 730.

[4] Compare Isa. xiv. 9, 10.

[5] Lenormant, *Beginnings*, 371 ; Sayce, *Hib. Lect.*, 395 ; Pinches,
Babylon. Ideas (Vic. Inst.), 5 ; *Expos. Times*, 1896, p. 207.

Similarly the tablet of the Seven Evil Spirits, at whose head stood Tiâmat[1]:

"In the first days the evil gods
The angels who were in rebellion, who in the lower
          part of heaven
Had been created,
They caused their evil work,
Devising with wicked heads."[2]

And again :

"Like lightning they darted,
     Descending to the abyss of waters."[3]

The fourth tablet of the Creation epic also mentions the punishment of the rebel gods (angels) who assisted Tiâmat :

"They bear their sin, they are kept in bondage.
And the eleven monsters are filled with fear.
As for the rest of the spirits who marched in her rear (?)
He laid cords on their hands. . . .
He fettered and laid the yoke on his foes . . .
Over the gods in bondage he strengthened his watch."[4]

Besides the foregoing should be placed a difficult passage in Isaiah (xxiv. 21, 22), which seems to bear a similar meaning : "The Lord shall punish the

[1] Smith, *Chald. Genesis*, 106, 98.

[2] G. Smith, *Assyr. Discoveries*, 398.

[3] Ibid., 399. The striking Babylonian passage in Isa. xiv. 12–15 should be compared, which speaks of the casting down of a heavenly potentate who rebelled against the Most High into the depths of Sheôl (Hell). The self-deification of the King of Babylon referred to was made an antitype of Satan and Anti-Christ (Delitzch, *in loco*). Compare S. Luke x. 18.

[4] Sayce, *Higher Criticism and the Monuments*, 68, 69.

host of the height on high. . . . And they shall be gathered together as prisoners are gathered in the pit, and shall be shut up in the prison. And after many days shall they be punished." The obvious import is that judgment will be visited by the Almighty on the army of His angels for some grievous offence on account of which they are thrust down into the pit as their prison.[1] The Book of Enoch carries on the tradition as follows: "There I saw a place beyond the great earth; there the waters collected. And I saw a great abyss in the earth . . . and over that abyss . . . a void place. The angel said, 'This is the place of the consummation of heaven and earth; it is a prison for the stars of heaven and for the host of heaven.'[2] 'These are of the stars who have transgressed the command of God the Highest, and are bound here till ten thousand worlds, the number of the days of their sins, shall have been consummated.'[3] 'This is the prison of the angels, and here they are held to eternity.'"[4] We have in these passages evidently the germ of the statement in the Second Epistle of

[1] So Rosenmüller, Delitzsch, &c. Instead of this passage being, as Gesenius thought, a proof of the later origin of the book, it preserves, as we see, an extremely ancient tradition.

[2] *Book of Enoch*, sect. iv. ch. 18, vv. 10, 12. 14 (ed. Schodde). He had already spoken of the *watery* nature of this abyss, ch. 17, vv. 5-8. The stars here seem equivalent to angels, as in Job xxxviii. 7 ; Isa. xiv. 12 ; *cf.* "wandering stars," Jude 13.

[3] *Book of Enoch*, ch. 21, v. 6.

[4] Ibid., v 10.

S. Peter (ii. 4), " God spared not angels who sinned,
but cast-them-down-to-Tartarus, and delivered them
over to caverns (σειροῖς, so the best MSS.) of darkness, reserved unto judgment ":—the caverns to
which they were consigned being, perhaps, those
of the watery abyss of Tartarus (Tĕhóm).[1]   The
employment of the essentially mythological word
ταρταρόω here is remarkable, it being used elsewhere
for the punishment inflicted by Zeus on Kronos and
the rebel Titans.[2]   It is interesting to note, moreover, that Kronos was identified by the Greeks with
Ea, the water-god, and the Titans with the Rephaim,
who occupied the subaqueous hell; while the word
Titan itself has been deduced from the Assyrian
Eta-ana, the ruler of Hades.[3]   The apostate angels
of S. Peter appear to be the same as those referred
to in Jude 6, who kept not their first estate, but
left their own habitation, and are reserved in everlasting chains under darkness; just as the Titans
were punished by Zeus (Hesiod, *Theog.*, 729).[4]   By

---

[1] Maitland notices that the overthrow of the fallen angels is
in some way connected with the deluge (*Eruvin*, 149, 155).

[2] Many of the Fathers thought that Titan was the mystic
name of the dragon-like beast in Rev. xiii. 18 (*Bible Dict.*, s. vv.
Giants, Titans).   The Titans are referred to in Judith xvi. 7.
See Plumptre, *in loco;* Böttcher, *De Inferis*, p. 79.

[3] Lenormant, *Chald. Magic*, 204 ; Sayce, *Hib. Lect.*, 195.

[4] Compare a very obscure account which Hippolytus gives of
the views of the Peratæ, a sect of heretics who, he says, were
imbued with Chaldaic influences.   They attributed importance
to " the power which is from Chaos "—" from the lowest depth
of mud "—" and has been called Thalassa (Sea) "   This power

a further and natural extension of the idea, the deep, which confined the evil spirits, was believed to be the place appointed for the punishment of wicked men also.

An Accadian folk-saw cautions the evil-doer with the words :

"If evil thou doest
To the everlasting Sea
Thou shalt surely go."[1]

11. **The Abyss.**—Tĕhôm, the Hebrew word for the chaotic waters in Gen. i. 2, is translated in the Septuagint by the word ἄβυσσος, abyss (Lat. *abyssus*), the great deep, and a good deal of its primeval significance clung to the term in its subsequent use in Biblical Greek.

"The sad black horror of Cimmerian Mists,
The sable fumes of Hell's infernall vault
(Or if ought darker in the world be thought)
Muffled the face of that profound Abyss,
Full of Disorder and fell Mutinies."[2]

---

ignorance has been accustomed to denominate Kronos, *guarded with chains because he tightly bound the fold of the dense and misty and obscure and murky Tartaros*" (*Refutation of All Heresies*, bk. v. ch. 9, Ante-Nic. Lib. i. 160–1).

[1] Sayce, *Folk-lore Journal*, i. 1883 ; or, "If evil thou hast done, to the Sea for ever thou goest" (*Records of the Past*, xi. 154). The Indian Varuna ("surrounder") is in the Purânas regent of the waters and the ocean personified, and as such "lord of punishment" (Goldstücker, *Lit. Remains*, 257).

[2] Sylvester, *Div. Weekes and Workes*, 1621, p. 7. A representation of Abyssus as personified is given in Didron, *Christian Iconography*, ii. 127.

In the New Testament it is used in a specific sense, as meaning either the region of the dead or the abode of evil spirits. Kurtz has noted that there is in Scripture a close mystical connection between the sea, and death, and Hades; Hengstenberg has made the same remark.[1] Accordingly we find in the Apocalypse the sea co-ordinated with Hades and Death, as a receptacle of the dead, which it delivers up at the Resurrection (Rev. xx. 13);[2] and S. Paul, as we have seen, uses Abyss as a synonym for Sheôl, the underworld of departed spirits.[3] In the Gospel of S. Luke the word is employed specifically for the abode of evil spirits in which they dread to be confined. The legion of demons entreated Jesus that He would not command them, when cast out of the man, to depart into the abyss (viii. 31); and yet

[1] Kurtz, *Old Covenant*, i. p. xxviii.; Hengstenberg, *Comm. on Rev.*, ii. p. 318. The Aryans also, as is well known, formed their name for the sea from a root *mar*, meaning to die; the Lat. *mare* being akin to the Sansk. *mara*, death. They probably conceived it as the watery waste; *cf.* Sansk. *maru*, a desert (M. Müller, *Science of Language*, ii. 352-3; C. F. Keary, *Primitive Belief*, 276).

[2] Hengstenberg, *in loco*. A medieval theologian, Antonius, Bishop of Florence, understood " the fishes of the sea " in Ps. viii. to be souls in Purgatory, and the breaking of the heads of the dragon in the waters (Ps. lxxiv. 13) to refer to the expulsion of demons in baptism (Farrar, *Hist. of Interpretation*, 297).

[3] Hence the patristic use of the word in the sense of Hades. S. Ambrose, *e.g.*, says of Christ, "Ipsa anima fuit in *Abysso*" (*De Incarn.*, cap. 5). The primitive Accadian *absu*, the Mystic Ocean, or great reservoir of waters, denoted also the abyss of the under-world.

when permitted to enter into the swine they proceeded under some irresistible impulse to rush headlong down into the sea, and so returned, no doubt, to their own proper abode beneath the waters. The abyss (ἄβυσσος) in this passage, as the haunt of evil spirits, corresponds, as Olshausen long ago remarked, to the Hebrew Tĕhôm, and, we may add, to Tĕhôm as inhabited by the demon-brood of Tiâmat.[1] With curious tenacity this ancient belief lived on in English folk-lore down to modern times. Evil spirits, when exorcised by priests or witches, according to the approved formula were banished to the bottom of the Red Sea. Dr. Johnson said that for his part he would rather lay a walking spirit in the tumultuous Buller of Buchan than in that time-honoured receptacle.[2] The word *abyss* occurs frequently in the Apocalypse in the same sense, as the dwelling-place of the devil and his angels, but unfortunately the Authorised Version has disguised the fact by rendering it " the bottomless pit; " the Revised Version correctly retains the word " abyss." In the 9th chapter, for instance (v. 11), the monstrous locusts " have over them as king the angel of the abyss; his

---

[1] Olshausen notices that Babylonian influences have been traced in the "popular notions" involved in the narrative of the Gadarene demoniacs (*Comm. in loco*).

[2] Brand, *Pop. Antiq.*, iii. 72, 85 ; Bassett, *Legends of the Sea*, 296 ; Addison, *The Spectator*, No. 12. The Roman rite of exorcism sends the evil spirit to keep company with Pharaoh and his host, whom God "in abyssum demersit" (*Notes and Queries*, III. xii. 56).

name in Hebrew is Abaddon (Perdition), and in the
Greek he hath the name Apollyon (Destroyer)." It
is out of the Abyss also that the various infernal
dragons of the vision are seen to arise, all legitimate
descendants of the aboriginal chaos-dragon, Tiâmat.
Owing to its use in the Vulgate in these passages,
Abyssus became a familiar word in Medieval Latin
for Hades and the infernal region.[1] From frequently
recurring in Mid-High German in the phrases *en âbis*
or *en obis* (= *in abysso*) it assumed the spurious form
nobis, in the sense of Orcus, death, or the under-
world, with many curious developments, such as
nobis-haus for purgatory (Hans Sachs), and *nobiskrug* (devil's-tavern) for hell (Luther). The rich
man's soul was in *nobiskrug* (Fischer).[2] Returning to
the Revelation, we find in the twelfth chapter (v. 3),
" the great red dragon having seven heads," which
vividly recalls its counterpart in a very early Babylonian hymn, " the huge serpent of seven heads, the
serpent that beats the sea, (which attacks) the foe in
the face, the devastator of forceful battle." [3] The
war that follows between this great Apocalyptic
Dragon with his angels and Michael and his angels
bears an unmistakable resemblance to the aboriginal

---

[1] "This pytte is the chyef and the manoyr of helle that is
clepid Abissus" (Lydgate, *Pylgr. Sowle*, 1483, iii. x. 56).

[2] See Kluge, *s. v.* Nobiskrug ; Grimm, *Teut. Myth.*, 805, 1002,
1605.

[3] Sayce, *Records of the Past*, xi. 128 ; *Hib. Lect.*, 282 ; Lenormant, *Chald. Magic*, 163, 232. Compare Shesha, the seven-headed
serpent of Brahma.

conflict between the Dragon Tiâmat, the leader of
the revolting powers of chaos and darkness on the
one side, and Merodach, the god of light and
champion of the heavenly powers, on the other;[1]
"the great overseer (or priest) of the spirits of
heaven," as he is called on one tablet.[2] And as we
find a few verses later (v. 9) that this heaven-defying
Dragon is expressly declared to be "the Old Serpent
that is called the Devil and Satan," we are confirmed
in the belief that Tiâmat is ultimately identical with
the Hebrew conception of Satan.[3] It is quite in
keeping that the Apocalyptic monster, as being
originally of oceanic origin, proceeds in his rage to
cast a river of water out of his mouth (v. 15).[4] We
may further compare Azi Dahâka, the three-headed
"fiendish snake" of the Zend-Avesta, the mightiest
demon created by the Evil Spirit, Angra Mainyu, to
destroy the world of the good principle. Striving to
seize and put out the *hvarenô*, the light of sovereignty
or glory from above, he is confounded and cast to
the ground.

It has been remarked that apocalyptic writers do

---

[1] Sayce, *Hib. Lect.*, 102, 283, 395.

[2] Ibid., 517.

[3] Grimm says that in early Teutonic legends the victory
of Christ over the infernal serpent was sometimes confused with
Thor's triumph over the world-snake, Iörmungandr (*Teut. Myth.*,
182).

[4] Boca del Drago, "Dragon's Mouth," was the name given by
Columbus to the dangerous surge in the Gulf of Paria (Taylor,
Names and their History, 112).

not invent their symbolism, but adapt it from early traditions;[1] and in particular, that primitive cosmogonic ideas were often employed in Christian times in an eschatological connection;[2] hence the Babylonian and Persian influences traceable in the Revelation.[3] W. Bousset has pointed out that the Antichrist legend is a later anthropomorphic resetting of the old Babylonian Dragon myth. "There existed in the popular Jewish belief the foreboding of another revolt of the old marine monster with whom God had warred at the Creation, who in the last days was again to rise and contend in heaven-storming battle with God. The expectation is not of any hostile ruler, but of a struggle of Satan directly with God, of a conflict of the Dragon with the Almighty throned in Heaven." "To me," says Bousset, "the Antichrist legend seems a simple incarnation of that old Dragon myth."[4] He shows in support of his contention that Antichrist is frequently represented as a dragon by Ephrem, the Sibyls, and

[1] W. Bousset, *The Antichrist Legend*, p. 6.

[2] Gunkel; *Crit. Rev.*, v. 262.

[3] Renan, *Antichrist*, ch. xvii. Gunkel thinks that he can even find "Primeval Chaos" (Heb. *Tĕhôm Qadmôniyyah*) in the mystical number 666 (p. 378).

[4] W. Bousset, *The Antichrist Legend*, 13, 144. "That opinion, that Antichrist should be born of the tribe of Dan" (Sir T. Browne, *Works*, ii. 367, after S. Augustine), originated in the prediction "Dan shall be a *serpent* in the way" (Gen. xlix. 17); this tribe is omitted in the enumeration of the "sealed" (Rev. vii. 5–8).

others,[1] or as a misshapen monster.[2] He maintains that Belial ("Badness"), otherwise Beliar (2 Cor. vi. 15), the opponent of Messiah and a wicked angel who rules the æthereal world (*Testam. Patriarcharum*, Dan. 5, and the Sibyls), is only another manifestation of the same ubiquitous Dragon.[3] The significant gloss of Hesychius is "Βελίαρ, δράκων."[4] In the following passage the word seems to be used for Satan or the Abyss of Destruction :

> " The cords of Death compassed me,
> And the floods of Belial made me afraid.
> The cords of Sheól were round about me " (Ps. xviii. 4).

The parallelism suggests that three infernal Powers are mentioned, and Jerome translated it "torrents of the Devil," Delitzsch "floods of the Abyss." The reference is perhaps to the river of the under-world, conceived as severing the living from the dead among many peoples."[5]

12. **Deserts as the Haunts of Devils.**—As the desolate waste of waters was believed to harbour evil spirits in its depths, in like manner upon earth

---

[1] W. Bousset, *The Antichrist Legend*, 145.

[2] Ibid., 156 : see *Bible Dict.*, iii. Appendix, lxxvii.

[3] Ibid., 136–7, 153-156.

[4] Ed. Schmidt, p. 371. Bengel interprets Belial to be Antichrist, and Böttcher as the Prince of Tartarus (*De Inferis*, 87, 88).

[5] *Cf.* Brinton, *Essays of an Americanist*, 146. So " A thing of Belial cleaveth to him "—Ps. xli. 8 (*i.e.*, a disease) seems parallel to S. Paul's " messenger of Satan " (2 Cor. xii. 7).

wildernesses and desert places, which seemed to be,
in the language of the peasantry, "God-forgotten"
spots, survivals standing over from the primeval
tohu va bohu, "wasteness and desolation," were
generally supposed to be the natural haunt of demons.
"In this world," says De Quincey, "there are two
forms of mighty solitude—the ocean and the desert;
the wilderness of barren sands and the wilderness of
the barren waters.¹ Both are the parents of inevit-
able superstitions—of terrors, solemn, ineradicable,
eternal."² An Accadian spell puts together "The
sea, the sea, The desert without water."³ In
Assyrian, Bahu, the great mother deep or water
of the chaotic abyss, was the home of the Seven
Evil Spirits, which seem to have been the destructive winds of the desert.⁴ They are described

¹ To the Aryan the sea (Lat. *mare*, "meer") and the desert
(Pers. *měru*, "moor") were both regions of death (Sk. *mara*,
mors); see C. F. Keary, *Contemp. Rev.*, Oct. 1879, p. 247.
Gizdhubar, inquiring his way to Xisuthrus, translated from
earth, says, "If it be suitable the *sea* let me cross, if it be not suitable the *desert* let me traverse" (Smith, *Chald. Genesis* (ed.
Sayce), 266). He has to pass over a great waste of sand and the
waters of death before he reaches the region of the blessed
(Ib., 329).

² *Works*, iii. 326. See his further remarks on the haunted
eeriness of deserts. *Cf.* Marco Polo (ed. Yule), i. p. xxxix. and
ch. 57, *sub init.*; Prejevalsky, *Mongolia*, i. 194; Burton, *Anatom.
of Melancholy*, I. 2, i. 2; Milton, *Comus*, 207-209; Sylvester, *Du
Bartas*, p. 274.

³ Lenormant, *Chald. Magic*, 10.

⁴ Sayce, *Hib. Lect.*, 199, 262.

as "the seven which unfold themselves in the earth, shaking the walls of the watery abyss."[1] Bohu, the wasteness of the unformed earth, corresponding to this among the Hebrews, it is probably due to this association of ideas that desert places, as representing what the whole world once was when ruined by the devil and his angels, came to be regarded by them as the congenial home of all evil things. "May the curse depart to the desert" is a frequent expression in Babylonian incantations.[2] Because in Assyrian belief, as Lenormant has noticed, evil beings had their habitual residence in uncultivated wilds and deserts, from which they wandered into inhabited places to torment mankind; accordingly there were special exorcisms with a view to sending them back to those dreary solitudes.[3] Indeed there was a general belief in Syria as well as Chaldea and Mesopotamia that demons inhabited the desert;[4] and there is ample evidence that the Jews inherited the same notion.[5] The scapegoat, loaded with the sins

---

[1] Lenormant, *Chald. Magic*, 28.

[2] Sayce, *Hib. Lect.*, 487, 476, 478, 526 ; Lenormant, *Chald. Magic*, 261 ; Ragozin, *Chaldea*, 156, 159.

[3] *Chald. Magic*, 31.

[4] Shakspere, in *Macbeth*, appropriately makes the powers of evil appear in a desert place with thunder and lightning ; it is a barren and blasted heath where evil has obtained the mastery of things (E. Dowden, *Study of Shakspere*, 249).

[5] So, among the Egyptians, Set or Typhon and Apap appear as evil demons dwelling in the desert (Kurtz, *Sacrific. Worship*, 400 ; Keary, *Prim. Belief*, 272 ; Ennemoser, *Hist. of Magic*, i. 179). The uninhabitable solitudes of Lapland were to the Finns

of the people, was sent away into the wilderness as
devoted to Azazel, the Evil One who dwelt in the
desert (Lev. xvi. 10).[1] Isaiah says that Babylon
shall become a ruin and desolation, so that "wild
beasts of the desert shall lie there, and the *sĕírím* [2]
(demoniacal beings like satyrs) shall dance there"
(xiii. 22). Of Edom, when laid waste, he says, "the
satyr shall cry to his fellow, and the night-monster
(Lilith) shall settle there" (xxxiv. 14); just as the
Apocalypse says of fallen Babylon, "It is become
a habitation of demons, and a hold of every unclean
spirit" (xviii. 2).[3] The devils, it is implied, have

what the burning sands of Arabia were to the Accadians, an
accursed country and a resort of foul spirits (Lenormant, *Chald.
Magic*, 245, 256). In the Old Persian religion Ahriman and his
evil spirits inhabit the steppes and wastes of Turan (Trench,
Studies in the Gospels, 7). *Cf.* the Jotunheim of N. Mythology;
Book of Enoch (ed. Schodde), p. 76.

[1] Keil, *Bib. Archæology*, ii. 43 ; Kurtz, *Sacrific. Worship*, 399.
So the sins of the people, when remitted, were cast into the
depths of the sea (Micah vii. 19), the seat of the evil principle,
like to like. "The regions in which the spirits of that con-
demned original population of the earth have taken their residence are the wastes, the deserts, the stormy winds, by which
the effects of their former power are symbolised" (Lange, *Life
of Christ*, ii. 44). See also J. Bonwick, *Egyptian Belief and
Mod. Thought*, 137.

[2] The Sĕírím of the desert were especially connected with
Babylon (Smith, *Chald. Genesis* (ed. Sayce), 205). They were not
to be worshipped : Lev. xvii. 7 ; Deut. xxxii. 17 (Ewald, *Antiquities
of Israel*, 223 ; Robertson Smith, *Relig. of the Semites*, 113, 114).
Similarly, the satyr-like Ṣabâni dwelt apart in the wilderness
(Ragozin, *Chaldæa*, 304).

[3] *Cf.* Baruch iv. 35. In Zechariah the woman, Wickedness

a malicious pleasure in all that is waste and desolate upon earth, in ruined paradises and overthrown
glory.[1]   Where the marks of the curse are most
apparent in barrenness, thorns and thistles, there
they exult and make their home.   In the Book of
Tobit, Asmodeus, the evil spirit, when exorcised by
Raphael, "fled into Upper Egypt," the type of a
waste and desolate land (viii. 3);[2] as in the Gospel
of S. Matthew (xii. 43) the unclean spirit, when
expelled from a man, in a similar manner wanders
through waterless or desert places, seeking in vain
for rest.   And finally, as Archbishop Trench remarks,
"this sense of the wilderness, as the haunt of evil
spirits, would of itself give a certain fitness to that,
as the place of the Lord's encounter with Satan,"
at the Temptation.[3]

13. **The Euphrates as a Spirit River.**—
There are sundry other traces of Babylonian ideas
pervading the symbolism of the Apocalypse which
would well repay examination, but we cannot enter
into the investigation here at any length.   I may
just indicate the difficult passage, Rev. ix. 14 *seq.*,

personified, is carried away, with the instruments of her un-
righteousness, to the Babylonian Shinar, the ideal land of
unholiness (vv. 6–8 ; see C. H. H. Wright, *in loco*).

[1] Stier, *Words of Jesus*, ii. 176.
[2] See Fuller, *Apocrypha, Speaker's Comm., in loco,* and p. 178.
[3] *Studies in the Gospels*, 7.   In a Rabbinic treatise Satan is
called the Prince of Tohu (Desolation) (Baumgarten, *Apost.
Hist.*, iii. 151); *Sheôl*, Hades, was sometimes identified with
Tohu (*Nineteenth Cent.*, "The Heb. Hell," No. 162, p. 271).

where four angels are said to be bound on the great
river Euphrates. The commentators, while recog-
nising in the binding a well-known allusion with
regard to evil spirits (*e.g.*, Book of Enoch x. 4; Tobit
viii. 3), have been at a loss to understand why the
Euphrates should be the place of their confinement.
We obtain some new light, however, when we learn
that in Babylonian belief the Euphrates, as being
the entrance to the great deep, Tehôm, was mystically
the point of contact with the spirit world; not only
was it the beginning of the ocean stream which was
supposed to encircle the earth like a monstrous
serpent,[1] but it was also identified with Datilla, the
River of Death, in the under-world.[2] Thus, while it
was called " the river of the great deep " and " the
river of the snake "[3] (viz., of the encircling ocean, of
which it was but a prolongation), it was called also
" the river of Innína," the mistress of the ghost-
world, and sometimes " the river of the sheep-cote
of the ghosts " (*subur lilli*), the latter expression
apparently meaning the place where spirits (*lil*)

[1] Sayce, *Fresh Light from the Ancient Monuments*, 42.

[2] Boscawen, *Sheol, B. M. Lectures*, ii. 17 ; Sayce, *Hib. Lect.*
359. Compare *supra*, p. 72.

[3] " The twisted serpent " of Isa. xxvii. 1 is understood to
mean the Euphrates with reference to its serpentine windings,
especially in the vicinity of Babylon (Delitzsch)—the " swift
flood . . . with serpent errour wandering " (*Paradise Lost*, vii.
302). Winding rivers in many countries take their names from
the serpent, *e.g.*, the Draco in Bithynia. The legend of the wood
of the cross tells of a great serpent coiled about a tree at the
source of the Euphrates (Grimm, *Teut. Myth.*, 1537).

were in safe-keeping).[1] The Euphrates, conceived
as Datilla, the River of Death, was the home of the
Annúnaki, or evil spirits, and the entrance to the
realm of Hades. In Lucian's *Necyomantcia*, Menippus
and his Chaldean guide embark on the Euphrates in
order to reach the land of the dead.[2] Here, perhaps,
we have also the origin of the enigmatical Domdaniel, the legendary submarine cavern at Babylon,
which was the abode of evil spirits and en-
chanters.[3]

> " In the Domdaniel caverns
> Under the roots of the Ocean
> Met the Masters of the Spell." [4]

---

[1] Sayce. *Hib. Lect.*, 116, 182, 281, 359. The Annúnaki, or
seven spirits of evil, inhabit the waters of death, whence they
issue as messengers of Allát and Death, in the guise of destructive winds (Maspero, *Hist. Ancienne*, 262). *Cf. Records of the
Past*, xi. 135.

[2] E. Smedley, *Occult Sciences*, 185.

[3] In the first sketch of Thalaba given by Southey, he speaks of
Domdaniel as a " seminary for evil magicians under the roots of
the sea," where they nurse earthquakes and feed volcanoes ; and
as the abode of the great serpent, and the spirit of Adam and
Nimrod (*Common Place Book*, iv. 182–189). There may be seen
" Eblis in giant form bearing up with one hand the arch of
Ocean, whose waves roll above its roof " (ib., 185).
> " The Domdaniel rock'd
> Through all its thundering vaults."
> (*Thalaba*, xii., xxiv.)

[4] Southey, *Thalaba*. He seems to have taken the name from
the French continuation of the *Arabian Nights* (1788–93).
Similarly the Muslims regard Babil as the fountain-head of
magic, which is taught there to mankind by two angels (or
magicians) in a great pit (Lane, *Selections from Kurán*, 118). I

The apocalyptic vision of the loosing of the destroying angels bound at the river Euphrates belongs, we cannot doubt, to this branch of the great Tiâmat cycle. An eschatological reference to the same is seen in the perilous water which, in the legends of all countries, the soul has to cross after death before it can win its way to its heavenly destination in the West. It is the Ocean-stream, separating this earth from the unknown Beyond, beneath which the Sun has his abode. The Spirit of the Waters, as the Spirit of Evil in the form of a monstrous dog or dragon, tries to seize and overcome the passing soul, and the Ocean-stream (Tiâmat), in which some are engulfed in the passage, becomes the abyss of hell.[1] For the righteous, however, a safe means of transit is provided. In the words of a curious death-chant used by the Badagas, a tribe in the Neilgherry Hills:

"The chamber dark of death
Shall open to his soul.

---

venture to think that Domdaniel or Dondaniel may be merely a perversion of Dên-dâin (= Heb. *Dîn-dayyân*, "Judgment of the Judge") in the Book of Enoch, 60, 8, the "void desert" cast of the Garden of Eden occupied by Behemoth. *Cf.* Dûdâ-el ("God's Kettle"), in which Azazel is confined (ib., 10, 4). Perhaps there is some connection with the Mohammedan tradition that Daniel dug out the Euphrates with the assistance of the angels (Evliya, *Travels*, iii. 110). Daniel was the master of the Babylonian magicians (Dan. iv. 9); he acts the part of Dante's Virgil in conducting a Rabbin over hell (*Nineteenth Cent.*, No. 162, p. 278).

[1] *Cf.* Brinton, *Myths of the New World*, 267.

> The sea shall rise in waves ;
> Surround on every side ;
> But yet that awful bridge
> No thicker than a thread,
> Shall stand both firm and strong.
> The dragon's yawning mouth
> Is shut—it brings no fear." [1]

The chief points which have come into prominence in the foregoing pages may be summed up as follows :

(1) The Mosaic record of the Creation is based on the more ancient accounts which have been preserved in the Babylonian tablets. In the words of Bishop Harold Browne, Moses probably had before him " the ancient primeval record of the formation of the world" and " certain documents or traditions referring to the patriarchal ages which he incorporated into his history." [2]   Or, as Renan puts it, Genesis i. embodies the Chaldean cosmogony as simplified by Semitic genius, and contains good Babylonian science for the time when it was written. [3]   There was a primitive religion of the whole Semitic race in which " El, 'The Strong One' in heaven, was invoked by the ancestors of all the Semitic races, before there were Babylonians in Babylon, Phenicians in Sidon and Tyrus, before there were Jews in Mesopotamia or Jerusalem." [4]   This was " the ancient

[1] C. E. Gover, *Folk-songs of S. India*, 75 ; Martinengro-Cesaresco, *Study of Folk-songs*, 391.

[2] *Speaker's Comm.*, i. 2 and 27.

[3] *Hist. of the People of Israel*, i. 67, 68.

[4] M. Müller, *Science of Religion*, 190.

common possession," says Professor Max Duncker, " of the Eastern Semitic tribes from whom the Hebrews were sprung;" but "with what clearness and vigour the Hebrews have succeeded in purifying and exalting the rude fancies of the nations so closely akin to them! The serious and thoughtful effort to deepen the traditions of the past into an ethical significance, to sublimate legends into simple moral teaching and transplant the myth into the region of moral earnestness and moral purpose—to pass beyond the rude naturalism of their kinsmen into the supernatural—from the varied polytheism of Babel and Canaan to monotheism—this it is which gives to the Hebrews the first place, and not among Semitic nations only, in the sphere of religious feeling and development."[1] The overruling and directing power which caused this spiritual development was inspiration.

(2) The religious conceptions of the Babylonians, which lay at the base of the Hebrews' early faith, in finding presentation and expression, seem to have had their *motif* or suggestion in some of the phenomenal aspects of Nature, more especially in that glorious sun-drama which has evoked the religious enthusiasm of most primitive peoples. Thus the primary idea of the operation of the Divine Creator was suggested by the Sun, the most potent and resplendent object in the natural world, which is the generator and source of all physical life and

Hist. of Antiquity, i. 287.

the apparent cause of all things that exist. Jehovah
Himself cannot be addressed by his worshipper in
fitter language than this: "The Lord God is a
sun" (Ps. lxxxiv. 11); nor His Messiah find a
loftier title than "the Sun of Righteousness"
(Mal. iv. 3). All spiritual conceptions, as is well
known, are founded on a material basis of this
nature. And "as the sun is the most striking
object in the firmament, the one source, as it
seems to the simple primitive mind, of light and
warmth, pure, exalted, potent, we need not wonder
that not only Moloch-worshippers, but seekers after
God in all lands and in all states of education, have
taken it as the image of the great and holy Being
after whom they seek, and developed their religious
vocabulary by ringing the changes on the phrases
that denote its unique qualities." [1]

(3) As the Babylonian sun-god, Merodach, the
Lord of Light, was held to be the Creator of the
Earth, so, on the other hand, the dark turbid waters
of the sea out of which the sun was seen to rise,
as if triumphant over a power that had held undisputed sway, became a vivid image of that primeval
chaos from which the world was called forth when
the Omnipotent subjugated it to law and order.

[1] Dr. J. Robertson, *Early Religion of Israel*, 247. He further
judiciously remarks that "it is simply impossible for man to use
language in regard to religious feelings and ideas without falling
into metaphor" (246); but " every so-called mythological *expression* is no indication of a mythological *belief* on the part of
the writer employing it " (191).

Accordingly the Great Deep was constituted a symbol of anarchy and lawlessness.

(4) This tumultuous water, the envelope of the Earth-mass, was personified as a dragon or serpentine monster, Tiâmat, and from being the representative of physical evil became ultimately significant of moral evil.

(5) Among the Hebrews this serpent or dragon is the being that introduces sin among the newly created race, and draws man into disobedience— i.e., to range himself on the side of the disorder and confusion of which the dragon-serpent in the cosmic sphere was the animated symbol, of which " the lawless one " (2 Thess. ii. 8), Antichrist, is to be the final development.[1]

(6) This Chaos-Dragon may be traced as an archaic survival and semi-mythological abstraction

[1] The following words of a sober writer in the *Quarterly Review* (vol. cxlvii, p. 319) deserve attention : " The increased acquaintance with primitive religions and their gradual developments, derived from their monumental and literary remains, has suggested such analogies and points of contact between them and ancient Hebraism, as to make the line of separation between them seem less sharp and clear than that which formerly appeared to divide a fabulous mythology from a supernatural revelation. Thus, there seems to be a growing persuasion that there is present throughout the Old Testament, in addition to the divine element of revelation, a real and large *humna element* mingled in varying proportions with the divine—an element by means of which its several parts, as they sprang into existence, were in vital contact with the language, thought, knowledge, moral and religious conceptions of the times in which respectively they originated."

in several books of the Old Testament. It further contributed shape and colouring to later conceptions of Satan or the Devil, who even down to mediæval times was believed to have some undefined connection with the great Deep, and was often called the Dragon.

(7) The Sea, as a visible remnant of the once universal waters of Chaos, upon which the Creator had to put forth His coercive powers, was held to be a rebellious element, hostile to law and order, and in league with the Spirit of Evil. As such it is eventually to be destroyed and have no place in the renovated earth.

(8) The Deep, or Abyss, as evil in itself and the unexplored home of mystery, was supposed to be the abode of evil spirits, and was identified with Hades, Tartaros, or Hell.

(9) Deserts and wildernesses, as the counterparts on land of the watery chaos, and typical survivals of the "waste and desolation" of the yet unformed earth, were similarly supposed to be the chosen haunt of evil spirits.

The ruling idea which runs through all these weird and sometimes grotesque conceptions is evidently that which Dr. Martineau has excellently developed in a thoughtful discourse on "The Realm of Order": "In the production and preservation of order all men recognise something that is sacred. We have an intuitive conviction that it is not, at bottom, the earliest condition of things; that whatever is, rose out of some dead groundwork of coufusion and nothingness, and incessantly gravitates thitherwards again ; and that, without a positive energy of God, no universe could have emerged from the void or be suspended out of it for an hour. There is no task more indubitably divine than the creation of beauty out of chaos, the imposition of law upon the lawless, and the setting forth of times and seasons from the stagnant and eternal night.[1] And so the Bible opens with a work of arrangement, and closes with one of restoration: looks round the ancient firmament at first and sees that all is good, and surveys the new heavens at last to make sure that evil is no more. . . . The spoiling of His works, the wild wandering from His will, He will bear no more ; the disorder that has gathered together shall be rectified ; He will again divide the darkness from the light, and confusion and wrong—all that hurts and destroys—shall be thrust into unknown depths ; while wisdom and holiness shall be as the brightness of the firmament, and as the stars for ever and ever."[2]

[1] Compare the splendid panegyrics on law in Hooker, *Eccles. Polity*, bk. i. § 3 ; Shakspere, *Tro. and Cress.*, i. 3, 83-130.

[2] *Endeavours after the Christian Life* (6th ed.), pp. 389, 390.

One of the Annúnaki, or demons of the Abyss (p. 59),
in attendance on Allât, the goddess of the Infernal
Region, represented as brandishing two serpents and
traversing Datilla, the River of Death (p. 77). From an
Assyrian monument (Maspero, *Histoire Ancienne*, p. 256).

APPENDIX

Note A.—The personification of the wild surging water of primæval chaos by the Babylonians as a dragon, serpent, or destructive monster, has analogies far and wide in the folk-lore of other nations. A few of these may here be enumerated :

(1) An impetuous torrent, winding its way down from the mountains and carrying away everything it meets in its course, is called in Switzerland a *drach* or dragon. The people of the Swiss Alps, says Grimm, preserve a number of traditions which tell of dragons that used to inhabit the mountains and often descend to commit ravages in the valleys. To this day, when a roaring torrent springs out of the depths of the forest and rushes headlong down the mountain, carrying with it trees and rocks, they are accustomed to say in a signiti-cant and proverbial way, "There's a dragon coming!"[1]

Naters, a village at the foot of the Simplon, which has often been laid waste by inundations, has a local legend that it was formerly infested by a dragon (Ger. *natter*, a snake), the memory of which is preserved in its name.[2]

[1] Grimm, *Veillées Allemandes*, i. pp. 355-357 (1838) ; *cf.* Chambers, *Book of Days*, i. 540.

[2] *Traditions et Légendes de la Suisse Romande*, 1872, p. 121 *seq.*

A cooper at Lucerne, in the year 1420, fell into a deep pit and passed the winter there in company with two frightful dragons, which took flight when they perceived that the winter was passed (*i.e.*, the torrents flowed when the snow thawed).[1]

Goruinuich, "Son of the Mountain" (Russ. *gora*), a name given in Russian folk-songs to the serpent (Zmyei), winged and many-headed,[2] seems similarly to indicate the mountain-sprung torrent. Another monster of the same people, the huge devouring Norka, is so called from its issuing out of a hole (*nora*);[3] and the Slavonic Neptune, Tsar Morskoi, or "King of the Waters," who is also the type of all evil, like Tiâmat, not only dwells in the depths of the sea as a winged serpent with many heads, but inhabits the mountain caverns [as the torrent]; he also carries off the daylight and the moon[4] (= when setting they are swallowed up in his waters).

The Archangel Michael, as being the typical conqueror of the dragon, was believed to have delivered Chonæ, the ancient Colosse, from an inundation of the Lycus, by appearing and opening a chasm in the earth for the waters to flow away.[5]

The "Dragon spring" (Neh. ii. 13) was so called

---

[1] Grimm, *op. cit.*, i. 356. Much about Swiss Dragons is to be found in J. J. Scheuchzer, *Itinera Alpina*.

[2] Ralston, *Songs of the Russ. People*, 173.

[3] Ralston, *Russian Folk-Tales*, 73.

[4] Ralston, *Russian Folk-Tales*, 65, 66, 115; *Songs of the Russ. People*, 148. Sadko, a kind of Slavonian Jonah, was cast overboard to pacify Tsar Morskoi (ib., 178). So to the Semite the monster of the sea devours the setting sun (Goldziher, *Myth. among the Hebrews*, 185).

[5] Hartley, *Researches in Greece*, 53 (see Lightfoot, *Ep. to Colos.*, 68, note 2).

because when its waters ebbed they were supposed to be swallowed up by a dragon, which haunted its source, and only permitted them to flow while he was asleep (Geikie, *Life of Christ*, ii. 93). So a dragon guarded the source of the river Ismenius, and another a fountain in Aulis (Bochart, *Opera*, ii. col. 439).

Gargouille, the dragon carried in the old rituals of Provence, was in like manner a personification of the demon of floods,[1] as at Arles a similar monster, Tarasque, was of the Rhone.[2] The latter has found its way to Lima, in the Southern Hemisphere.[3]

When the flood of an overflowing river is confined within its banks the Chinese say " the dragon is caged " (N. B. Dennys, *Folk-Lore of China*, 108).

The Egyptian serpent, likewise, is sometimes a symbol of water or floods (Lenormant), and the Hydra or water-serpent of Lerna, which was overcome by Hercules, is of the same brood; unless, indeed, like some mediæval dragons, it represented miasmatic exhalations.[4]

Other awe-inspiring phenomena of a meteorological character are personified in the dragons of mythology.

(2) The Hebrew *tannîn*, or leviathan (Ps. cxlviii. 7), as well as the Arab *tinnîn* (sea-monster), represents the

---

[1] Compare " gargoil," Sansk. *giryara*, whirlpool, Lat. *gurges*. Didron, *Christ. Iconography*, ii. 115, 259; Chambers, *Book of Days*, i. 540.

[2] Martinengo-Cesaresco, *Study of Folk-Songs*, 186.

[3] Hampson, *Kalendarium Medii Aevi*, i. 219. He refers to an article on the dragon of Metz by M. Lenoir in *Mém. de l'Académie Celtique*, tom. ii. See T. Wright, *Essays on Archæology*, i. 238 seq.

[4] F. E. Hulme, *Mythland*, 30. Perhaps the Dragon of Wantley and the Lambton Worm belong here. See also further dragon stories in A. C. Fryer, *Eng. Fairy Tales from the N. Country*, 1896; Busk, *Sagas from Far East*, 384; *Household Stories from Land of Hofer*, 348.

water-spout.[1]   The Chinese regard the same phenomenon as a serpent of the abyss rising towards heaven, and call it "the Dragon King of the Deep"[2] (cf. Job vii. 9). The chronicler John of Brompton describes a water-spout as a great black dragon with his tail turned to the sky and his head drinking up the water.[3] Anyi-ewo, the Rainbow God of the Slave Coast, somewhat similarly is represented as "the Great Snake from Underneath," which comes up to drink.[4] The Japanese also hold the water-spirit to be a dragon.[5]

The serpent form so commonly attributed to the encircling ocean has been referred to above.   It is represented as running round an ancient Phœnician patera found at Præneste :[6]

> "Methinks, when tempests come and smite the Ocean
> Until the vast and terrible billows wake,
> I see the writhing of that curled snake
> Which men of old believed."[7]

Professor Cheyne is of opinion that the sea-monster which swallowed up Jonah was Rahab, "the Raging One" (i.e., the storm-dragon);[8] and Steinthal thinks that it is the same monster which in Job xxvi. 11–13 devours the sun and light of the sky and is destroyed by Jahveh.[9]

---

[1] Robertson Smith. *Religion of the Semites*, 161 ; cf. Kuenen, *Nat. and Universal Religions*, 316.

[2] S. R. Maitland, *False Worship*, 275.

[3] See Baring-Gould, *Book of Werewolves*, 173; F. S. Bassett, *Legends of Sea*, 30–33 ; P. Sébillot, *Légendes de la Mer*, ii. 116 seq.

[4] A. B. Ellis, *Ewe-speaking Peoples of W. Africa*, 47–49.

[5] P. Sébillot, *Légendes de la Mer*, ii. 117.

[6] Rawlinson, *Phœnicia*, 229.

[7] Barry Cornwall, *Eng. Songs*, 1844. p. 205.

[8] *Theolog. Review*, 1877. p. 215.

[9] Goldziher, *Myth. among the Hebrews*, 423.

Legends of aquatic monsters which frequent lakes in the form of a dragon or serpent abound in ancient Irish folk-tales.[1] Thus, Fergus, King of Ulster, had a conflict with a frightful sea-monster, Muirdris, in the bottom of Loch Ruaighre.[2] In another old Irish legend Rosualt is an ocean-dwelling monster which produces dearth when it turns its face to land.[3] That obscurely mysterious dragonlike creature, Grindel's Mother, whom Beówulf slew, " dwelt in the fearful waters, cold streams." [4]

The Ojibiways have a legend of a great serpent infesting the waters of a deep lake.[5] A myth current among the Algonkins and Iroquois tells of a similar monster which dwells in their great lakes, and unless appeased with offerings raises a tempest and swallows down those that intrude on his domain.[6] The Hurons imagine that a serpent of huge size, called Angont, which sends sickness, death, and other mishaps, dwells in the lakes and rivers ;[7] and Servian folk-lore has a dragon, Ajdaya, which lurks in the waters of a lake.[8]

In South France the Drac, a supernatural being that, according to Gervase of Tilbury, had its abode in the caverns of rivers, and used to drag down any person who came within its reach, was a survival of the *draco* or

Joyce, *Irish Names of Places*, i. 189–192.

P. Kennedy, *Bardic Stories of Ireland*, 61.

[3] Forgaill, *Amra Choluim Chilli* (ed. Crowe), 45.

[4] *Beówulf*, ll. 1261–2.

[5] Squier, *Serpent Worship of America* (F. E. Hulme, *Mythland*, 163 seq.).

[6] D. G. Brinton, *Myths of the New World*, 113.

Ibid., 143.

Ralston, *Russian Folk-Tales*, 111.

dragon.[1] The Drakos of modern Greek popular tales,
which, like the last mentioned, has a human form and in
some respects resembles the Norse troll, is of the same
origin; though some tales give evidence of its rather
having been the thunderstorm.[2] In one Greek folk-
song the Drakos exclaims: "I'm the Lightning's son,
And she is daughter of the Thunder."[3]

(3) Ewald remarks that, while the serpent was
originally the beast of the abyss, dismal, ferocious and
frightful, "as the imagination figured to itself the
outermost abyss of the universe inhabited by a huge
serpent, a dragon, so a similar monster was supposed
suddenly to fill the lower heavens in the black thunderstorm."[4] Mr. Baring-Gould had already arrived at the
same conclusion: "The dragon of popular mythology is
nothing else than the thunderstorm, rising at the
horizon, rushing with expanded, winnowing, black
pinions across the sky, darting out its forked fiery
tongue and belching fire."[5] To the ancients the forked
and writhing lightning seemed as a heavenly fiery
serpent.[6] "What a glorious snake was that!" said a
German peasant as a vivid forked gleam shot to earth.[7]
The Shawnees make identically the same remark,[8] and
the Red Man too sees in the darting lightning a fiery

[1] Keightley, *Fairy Mythology*, 465; Hartland, *Science of Fairy Tales*, 65.
[2] H. F. Tozer, *Researches in the Highlands of Turkey*, ii. 293–303.
[3] L. M. J. Garnett, *Greek Folk-Songs*, 12, 79.
[4] *Revelation*, p. 226. He refers to the Sanskrit *Ahis buhdnjds*, "the serpent or dragon of the abyss" (p. 227).
[5] *Book of Werewolves*, 172.
[6] Euripides, *Herc. Fur.*, l. 395.
[7] Baring-Gould, *Werewolves*, 171.
[8] *Fortnightly Review*, April 1894, p. 537.

serpent or dragon.[1] Indeed, the "cherubim" and "seraphim"[2] of the Old Testament are now generally considered to be personifications respectively of the dragonlike storm-clouds and the serpentine lightnings.[3] The two *livyâthâns* of Isa. xxvii. 1 are interpreted to be the storm-clouds and darkness;[4] and "the flying serpent" of Job xxvi. 12, 13, is the lightning (Isa. xiv. 29).[5] The seven wicked spirits which attack the moon, and are called "Serpents of Death" on a Babylonian tablet, are the storm-clouds.[6] The dragon-headed Typhœus (Hesiod, *Theog.*, 870 *seq.*) is the hurricane, and the monstrous-winged Harpies, which carried off people suddenly, are the whirlwinds.[7] M. Maury notes that the elongated form which clouds and mists often take as they wind ("serpentent") through the atmosphere appeared to the early Aryan as a huge reptile ready to swallow up the sun. Hence the great dragon Ahi of the Vedas, residing in the air at the source of the rivers, and Vritra, which Indra slays with his thunderbolts.[8] Even so in Accadian belief the devastating tempest and the darkening eclipse were irruptions of the original chaos of anarchy and gloom into the fair

[1] Brinton, *Myths of the New World*, 117, 125.

[2] The Seraphim appear as Chalkidri in the *Book of Secrets of Enoch*, xii. 1, where they have the form of huge serpents (ed. Charles, p. xxx.), and are called δρακόντες in the Greek of the Ethiopian *Enoch*, xx. 7.

[3] So Riehm; Ewald, *Prophets of O. Test.*, ii. 70; Cheyne, *Isaiah*, i. 37; Robertson Smith, *Prophets of Israel*, 218; Delitzsch, *New Comm. on Genesis*, i. 174; Goldziher, 197.

[4] Cheyne, *in loco*.

[5] Goldziher, 185.

[6] Sayce-Smith, *Chald. Genesis*, 102, 114; *Bab. Literature*, 35.

[7] F. Paley, Ovid, *Fasti*, v. 204.

[8] *Croyances et Légendes de l'Antiquité*, 105-108; cf. Bassett, 229 *seq.*

order of nature;[1] and in the Indian mythology it is a dragon of darkness, Rahu, that preys upon the sun and moon.[2] The Caribs conceive the god of the thunder-storm as a great serpent dwelling in the forests, and in the Quiché legends " the Strong Serpent," " He who hurls below," are names for Hurakan, the hurricane, or thunderstorm.[3] The Mexicans and other tribes of the New World worshipped Mixcoatl, " the Cloud Serpent," or Iztac-Mixcoatl, " the Gleaming Cloud Serpent," both personifications of the tropical tornado.[4] Among the Chinese every cloud with a curious configuration or serpentine tail is a dragon, and the scattering of the cloud is his disappearance.[5] " There is the dragon," says Confucius ; " I cannot tell how he mounts on the wind through the clouds and rises to heaven."[6] Lung, the flying Saurian, which is the ruler of the clouds and sends rain and floods, lies hidden in the marshes and watery depths during the winter, and in the spring ascends to the skies.[7] This is the dragon which has become the national emblem of China. Similarly the Egyptian snake, Apophis, the enemy of the sun-god, represents the storm-cloud,[8] as on Aryan ground does Ahriman in antagonism to Mithra, and Zohak paired

1 Sayce, Hib. Lect., 333.

2 Goldstücker, Lit. Remains, i. 151.

3 D. G. Brinton, Myths of the New World, 119.

4 Ibid., 171.

5 Du Bose, The Dragon. Image and Demon, 317. Cf. " Sometimes we see a cloud that's dragonish," Shaks., Ant. and Cleop., iv. 12, 3. " Do you see yonder cloud that's almost in shape of a camel? . . . . or like a whale?" Hamlet, iii., 2, 392-8.

6 Du Bose, 347.

7 Edkins, Study of Chinese Characters, 39, 135 ; Du Bose, 315, 316.

8 Ball, Speaker's Comm., Apocrypha, ii. 356.

against Feridun ;[1] and so among the Russians Yegory
(= St. George) contending with the serpent denoted
originally the spring-tide struggle between Perun, the
Thunder-god, and the dark storm-clouds of retreating
winter, which he pierces with his lightning shafts.[2]
Winter itself, among the latter people, conceived as an
evil spirit which wars against sunlight and fair weather,
has taken the form of a snake, and is dreaded as the
demon Koshchei, " the ossifying," which hardens what
it touches.[3] In the same manner the dragons which
formerly used to be borne in the church processions of
Rogation-tide—i.e., in the middle of spring—were
emblematic of winter, as overthrown by the vernal sun,
and so of the victory of light over darkness, of the
beneficent principle over the principle of evil.[4]

(4) An old name for a dragon in English was *drake*
(Anglo-Saxon *draca*, Lat. *draco*, Mod. Gk. *drakos*,
the *drac* or evil spirit of the Rhone), and various fiery
meteors or phenomena that left a luminous trail behind
them used to be popularly known as " Fire-Drakes " or
" Flying Dragons."[5] The Esthonian peasant in similar
phraseology, when he sees red streaks in the sky, says
" the dragon is setting out," and shooting-stars he calls
" little dragons."[6] Beówulf has *fýr-draca*, l. 2690.

---

[1] *Cf.* also Frode's and Fridleif's contest with dragons, *Saxo-Grammaticus* (Folk-lore Soc.), 45, 222.

[2] Ralston, *Songs of the Russ. People*, 233.

[3] From Russ. *Kost'*, a bone (ib., 166).

[4] R. T. Hampson, *Kalendarium Medii Aeri*, i. 219.

[5] Nares, s.v. Fire-drake ; T. Hill, *A Contemplation of Mysteries* (ab. 1590); *Wonderful Hist. of Storms*, 1704, p. 66; Brand, *Pop. Antiq.* (Bohn), i. 321 ; ii. 411. See Nisard, *Hist. des Livres Populaires*, i. 110.

[6] Grimm, *Teut. Myth.*, iv. 1847.

In a thirteenth-century poem Satan is called "the fire-burning drake" :

> "Ther is Sathanas the qued [evil]
> redi wyth his rake ;
> And so me wile for-swolewe
> the fur-bernynde drake."
>
> *Old Eng. Miscellany* (E. E. T. S.), p. 181.

It is, no doubt, from some confusion with this ancient meaning of the name that the famous old sea-dog Sir Francis Drake has been partly mythologised and diabolised in folk-lore. There were long current traditions in Devonshire that Drake had dealings with the devil and owed his success to diabolic assistance.[1] With the help of his demon he is reputed to have drawn the waters in a channel from Dartmoor to Plymouth, and at Devil's Point hard by to have created gunboats out of logs of wood. "On every hand," says Mr. Robert Hunt, "we hear of Drake and his familiars."[2] A faded far-off reminiscence this of the Dragon of the Deep, grown round the name of the great sea-warrior.

Curiously enough, the *nomen* of the redoubtable admiral was similarly interpreted as an *omen* by his Spanish enemies.[3] Lope de Vega wrote a poem, *La Dragontea* (1598), with the motto " Conculcabis leonem et *draconem*" —Ps. 90, in which he represents Drake (Francisco Draque) as the instrument of Satan, referring to him as " el *Draque* Ingles," " Capitan *Dragon* famoso " (p. 35).

---

[1] Mrs. Bray, *The Tamar and the Tavy*, letter 27 ; Southey, *Letters*, iv. 260, 342 ; *Notes and Queries*, III., viii. 223.

[2] *Romances and Drolls of the West of England*, i. 261.

[3] The surname Drake, no doubt, actually meant " dragon " originally, as we find in old records Walter le Dragon as well as Adam le Drake (Bardsley, *Eng. Surnames*, 543).

" Quiso en el alma del *Dragon* Francisco
Infundir por sus ojos basilisco " (p. 33).

The reader will notice that many passages in the Authorised Version which mention " dragons " have not been referred to in the essay—*e.g.*, " Thou hast sore broken us in the place of *dragons* " (Ps. xliv. 19); " Babylon shall become a dwelling-place for *dragons* " (Jer. li. 37). The word translated so is in the Hebrew *tannim*, which means " jackals " (distinct from *tannin*, dragons). It occurs also in the following references: Job xxx. 29 ; Isa. xiii. 22 ; xxxiv. 13 ; xxxv. 7 ; xliii. 20 ; Jer. ix. 11 ; x. 22 ; xiv. 6 ; xlix. 33 ; Micah i. 8 ; Mal. i. 3.

A few disconnected annotations here follow :

Philo speaks of the tempter in the Garden as " a *dragon* (δράκων) uttering the voice of a man."[1]

Propertius (bk. v. 8) tells of an aged Dragon that was of old time the guardian of Lanuvium, in whose honour a maiden used occasionally to be let down into his cavern.

The figure of a dragon as an awe-inspiring creature was from the earliest times carried before an army.

In commenting on Barbour's line—

" [They] byrn, and slay and raiss *dragoun* "
(*The Bruce*, ii. 11)

—Prof. Skeat notes that the phrase means to set up the standard, which was originally in the form of a dragon ; as, indeed, it was even in ancient Egypt (see Sharpe, *Egypt. Mythology*, p. 36). The old French phrase for to undertake a campaign was " faire voler le dragon " (De

Works, trans. Yonge, i. 398. Compare d'Alviella, *Migration of Symbols*, 166.

Lincy, *Proverbes Français*, ii. 600). See Du Cange, *s.vv.* Draco, Draconarius. Of the same origin is our " dragoon."

J. J. Scheuchzer, *Itinera Alpina* (1723), gives eleven gruesome figures of Swiss dragons (pp. 377-397). He quotes Carpzov as having shown from Rabbinical writers that the Jews were forbidden to engrave the form of the dragon (p. 377). For much further dragon-lore and illustrations, see Charles Gould, *Mythical Monsters*, 212 *seq.*, 377 *seq.*, 392 ; *Notes and Queries*, I. ii. 517, III. ix. 158, 266, 497, IV. vii. 125, 477 ; Pliny, *Nat. History*, viii. chh. 13, 14.

For their prehistoric prototypes, see Prof. O. C. Marsh's monograph on the Dinosaurs (U. S. Geolog. Survey, 1897). N. B. Dennys, *Folk-Lore of China*, ch. x., and Collin de Plancy, *Dict. Infernal* (1863), 220, may also be consulted.

Note B.—Merodach, the Vanquisher of the Chaos-Dragon, and so Creator of the ordered world, as being originally the Sun-God, occupied a place of supreme importance in the Babylonian religion, and by a reflex influence seems to have contributed shape to the theological conceptions of the Jews both as to the God-head and the Logos.

In the prehistoric Accadian system his name was Amar-utuki, " The Brightness of the Sun,"[1] and inasmuch as that luminary appears to rise out of the sea, he was held to be the son of Ea, the god of the

---

[1] Tiele, *Hist. of Anct. Religions*, 68 ; Lenormant, *Chald. Magic*, 132 ; Pinches, *Rel. Ideas of Babylonians*, 2 ; *Trans. Soc. Bib. Arch.*, iii. 140.

deep, "The first-born of the Deep."[1] As the genial
solar deity he was revered as the benefactor of mankind,
and as the mediator between God and man,[2] his customary
title being "Giver of good to Men" (Silik-mulu-Khi), or
"The Prince who does good to Man" (Asari-uru-dug).
Among the Babylonians and Assyrians Amar-utuki
or Amar-uduk became contracted into Maruduk and
Marduk (and later Merodach), and it appears to have
been understood as Amar-udug, "Gazelle of the day,"[3]
another Semitic form of the name being Amar-ud, which
means "heifer (or hind) of the day." [4] These are
known to have been poetical expressions among the
Semites for the rising sun, and would therefore be appropriate appellations of the solar god. The Arabs speak
of the sunrise as " the rising of the gazelle" (al-gazâlâ),[5]
the spreading rays of the sun being to the Semitic mind
suggestive of an animal's horns (Assyr. *Karni;* Heb.
Keren).   Our own Jeremy Taylor says that the sun

[1] Sayce, *Hib. Lect.*, 460.
[2] Tiele, 69 ; Lenormant, 100; Sayce, 106.
[3] So Hommel; Schrader, *Cuneiform Inscr.*, ii. 116.
[4] Sayce, *Hib. Lect.*, 106.
[5] Goldziher, *Myth. among Hebrews*, 178. Similarly in Accadian the
sun-god at Sippara was called Uz, *i.e.,* " The Goat." Al Ozza, or al
Uzza, the goddess which, according to the old tradition (*supra*, p. 2),
Abraham worshipped in his days of heathendom, was a deity of the
Ancient Arabs, especially the Koreish, and is mentioned in the Korân
(ch. 53). See Sale, *Prelim. Discourse*, pp. 13 and 380 (ed. 1850). Uzza is
said to signify " the Mighty One," and the name has been found on a
stone image of a cow and a calf (Duncker, *Hist. of Antiquity*, i. 329,
330). She was apparently the feminine form of the Babylonian Uz, a
deity who is explained to be " the (great) spirit" and the sun-god.
The original idea of the name was perhaps "the horned one" (as
above), since the Accadian Uz means "a goat," and it is called " the
long-horned " (Sayce, *Hib. Lect.*, 284-5).

"peeps over the eastern hills, thrusting out his *golden horns*, like those which decked the brows of Moses."[1] Compare Karneios, a name of Apollo, as the ray-diffusing sun-god. Similarly Merodach was called "the mighty one of the gazelle god," and two horned animals were sacred to him; as a tablet expresses it, "The wild goat and the gazelle were protected by him."[2]

As we find the same figure occurring in the Babylonian Talmud, where the first appearance of light is called "the hind of the morning's dawn," because it is "like two horns of light rising from the east,"[3] we may trace a connection between this ancient religious usage and the somewhat enigmatical title prefixed to Psalm xxii., "Upon the Hind of the Dawn" (*Al Ayyeleth hashshachar*). A Messianic reference was perhaps recognised in the ancient Babylonian phrase "Hind of the Dawn," as originally applied to the mediatorial god, Merodach; and the manifestation of the Messiah was, as so often, compared to the benign influence of the rising sun. At all events, Jerome understood the Hind of the Dawn to be "no other than Christ Himself."[4] It has often been remarked that Merodach, as mediator, healer and redeemer, as forgiving sin, defeating the tempter, and

[1] *Works*, 1828, iv. 350. On St. Jerome's unfortunate rendering of Heb. *Káran*, to put forth (1) horns, (2) rays, in Exod. xxxiv. 29, as "cornutam (faciem)," see A. S. P., *Folk-Etymology*, 177. Compare "pectines solis," which, according to Tertullian, African nurses used to sing about (*Cont. Valentin.*, cap. iii.); Cassell, *Esther*, 383.

[2] Boscawen, *Bible and Monuments*, 78, 80.

[3] Delitzsch, *Psalms*, vol. ii. p. 308; Low and Jennings, *Psalms*, vol. i. p. xv.

[4] "In the very Front or Inscription of this Psalme our Saviour Christ is compared *Cerro matutino* to the morning Hart" (Bp. Andrewes, xcvi. *Sermons* (1628), p. 334). If, as many think, the title

raising the dead, in many of his features foreshadowed the Hebrew Messiah.[1] Indeed, the Babylonians themselves seem to have considered their Merodach (or Bel) and the Hebrew Ya (Jah = Jehovah) to be one and the same, as we may infer from the names they gave their children, such as Bel-Yahu—i.e., "Bel is Ya," identical with Bealyah, the name of one of David's warriors (1 Chron. xii. 5); and Shamshi-Ya, "My Sun is Ya."[2] It is remarkable, too, that the two typical Jews and protagonists of the Book of Esther, Mordecai and Esther, bear the names of the Babylonian deities, Merodach (Marduk) and Istar. Professor Cheyne has expressed his belief that the Jews had their religious ideas stimulated and exalted by becoming acquainted with Marduk and the lofty conceptions attached to him.[3] Mr. Pinches has further shown that Merodach was recognised as being the supreme deity of which many others were only particular manifestations.[4] Among other titles given to him on the monuments are the following: "The first-born, the glorious, the first-born of the gods, Merodach, the prince;"[5] "Filling heaven and earth;" "The merciful one who loves to

is that of an ancient melody, the reference may still be the same, as it would be the words of the ancient song that gave a name to the tune, like our "Green Sleeves," "Packington's Pound," &c.

[1] See H. E. Ryle, *Early Narratives of Genesis.*

[2] Pinches, *Rel. Ideas of the Babylonians,* 12, 13.

[3] *Nineteenth Century,* Dec. 1891, pp. 954, 964.

[4] *Op. cit.,* 10, 11. Merodach has many features in common with Quetzalcoatl, the fair and gentle god of the Aztecs, who was also a solar deity (Brinton, *Essays of an Americanist,* 84 *seq.*; Prescott, *Conquest of Mexico,* 70th ed., 19, 464; Tylor, *Ear   Hist. of Mankind,* 153 (3rd ed.).

[5] Sayce, *Hib. Lect.,* 97.

raise the dead to life;"[1] "He who maketh whole;"[2]
"Creator of the universe;"[3] "Revealer of the spirits of
heaven;"[4] "The only begotten one;"[5] "The omniscient
lord of heaven and earth, the creator of the law of the
universe;"[6] "Life;"[7] "Restorer of their benefit" (to
the fallen).[8]

Among the characteristics which qualify him to be
compared with Michael, the Lord of angels, in addition
to his overthrow of the Dragon, are these which follow :
"All the angel-hosts of heaven and earth Regard thee
and give ear;"[9] "The great overseer of the spirits of
heaven;"[10] "the king of the angels;"[11] "the director of
the spirits of heaven."[12]

Christ Himself (of Whom I hold Michael to be an
official manifestation in His relation to the angels) is
represented on a Gnostic seal in the British Museum as
trampling on a Saurian monster.[13]

> "Tu l'as mal écrasé, Christ, ce reptile immonde
> Que toute vérité trouve sur son chemin !
> De ses hideux replis il enlace le monde,
> Et son dard profond reste aux flancs du genre humain."[14]

Professor Robertson evidently goes too far when he
asserts that " there is no Semitic god of the dawn, nor in
the Hebrew Scriptures any hint of the contest of light
with darkness;"[15] but we need not differ from him when

---

[1] Sayce, *Hib. Lect.*, 99.   [2] Id., 502.   [3] Id., 100.

[4] Id., 128, 149.   [5] Id., 144.   [6] Id., 537.

[7] Pinches, *Rel. Ideas*, 5.   [8] Boscawen, *Bible and Monuments*, 89.

[9] Sayce, 99, 502.   [10] Id., 517.

[11] Id., 508 (l. 95).   [12] Id., 537.

[13] W. R. Cooper, *Serpents of Egypt*, 71.

[14] Lamartine, *Harmonies* (1863), p. 294.

[15] *Early Religion of Israel*, 505.

he goes on to maintain that "the Hebrew writers, from the earliest point we can reach them, though saturated with poetry, are free from mythology in the ordinary sense."[1] So are we modern Christian Englishmen when we use terms like "jovial," "mercurial," "saturnine;" but, without some knowledge of the Roman mythology which underlies them, those words would be inexplicable. It is not always easy, either, to sharply divide between the mythological and the metaphorical.

From a wide comparative survey of the religions of the world, Professor Tiele concludes that it was not only on the Semites, but indirectly on the nations of the West, that the religion of the Accadians exercised a powerful influence.[2]

P. 35. The symbol of the thunderbolt, resembling two tridents bound together back to back, with which Merodach is depicted on the monuments as overcoming Tiâmat (see frontispiece), seems to represent lightning streaming from a cloud, and is much more true to nature, as revealed by instantaneous photography, than the conventional zigzag of modern art. If I mistake not, we may find here the origin of a symbol which in various related forms was widely diffused among the Aryan nations. It has been touched on by Count Goblet d'Alviella in his learned work on "The Migration of Symbols." In a form but slightly different, that of a bifid sheaf denoting a thunderbolt, it appears on a prehistoric terra cotta from Troy on each side of a head of Assyrian style.[3] The same figure is preserved in the

[1] *Early Religion of Israel,* 506.
[2] *Hist. of the Ancient Religions,* 68.
[3] See Schliemann, *Ilios,* p. 617, and tablet 1460, p. 618.

dordj,[1] a symbol used by the Buddhists in China and Japan to exorcise demons. It is to be traced in the winged fulmen of Greek coins of the fifth century B.C., *e.g.*, on the stater of Elis (see plates of Bunbury Collection Sale, 1896, Nos. 1084, 1087 ; also 72, 222, 471, 499, 827).

We also find ⊔⊔, a trident or pitchfork, used as a Chaldean symbol for lightning,[2] and this is evidently only a halving or abbreviated form of the original. It is "the flame of the turning weapon" which guarded the gate of Eden (Gen. iii. 24).

Of the same meaning, no doubt, is the emblem ⊔⊔ frequently occurring on the whorls of ancient Troy, sometimes in conjunction with zigzags, another form of lightning;[3] found also above the door of hut-urns discovered at Alba Longa,[4] perhaps as an amulet to defend the hut from lightning; and on the tomb of the Irish king Ollam Fodhla.[5] If this symbol was used, as is likely, as distinctive of the god of the sky, in the same way that the thunderbolt was characteristic of Zeus and Jupiter, and the runic cross or hammer (the thunderbolt) was of Thor,[6] we get a new light on the enigmatical gnomic

---

[1] D'Alviella, *Migration of Symbols*, 99 and 97. Compare also ‡ a German symbol of the thunderbolt put on stables (Gubernatis, *Mythologie des Plantes*, i. 26, note 1).

[2] D'Alviella, 97, 98.

[3] Schliemann, *Ilios*, figs. 1905, 1912, 1936, 1939, also 1408 (p. 601).

[4] I. Taylor, *Origin of the Aryans*, 176.

[5] Schliemann, p. 350.

[6] G. Stephens, *Thunor the Thunderer*, 16, 33 *seq.*; Zoeckler, *Cross of Christ*, 20.

saying of the Greek poet Callias in the prologue to his drama called *Grammar* (fifth century B.C.), " E belongs to God " (Θεοῦ γὰρ εἶ γε). It is a play, I venture to think, on an older formula, " ⊔⊔ is the prerogative of deity "—none but he can wield the thunderbolt. This is the more probable, as the letter E in the Cypriote alphabet has the form ✳, agreeing closely with the Babylonian symbol for the thunderbolt.[1] It would also help to explain the famous and much-debated " E of Delphi." Plutarch mentions that Ei (the name of the letter E) was inscribed on the doors of the temple of the oracle there, and wrote a curious but inconclusive treatise on its probable signification.[2]

Like the Є found on a Gnostic gem with the legend PVCOV ("Thou wilt protect "),[3] it was an amulet to avert lightning or other danger.

Of the same origin is ⫸ and ∠, a symbol of the thunderbolt on Trojan pottery;[4] the arrow of Perkun,

[1] See Sayce in Schliemann's *Ilios*, pp. 702 and 693 ; and compare the Trojan letter E on seal (ibid.). Vajra, Indra's weapon, the thunderbolt, shaped like an X or decussated cross (D'Alviella, *Mig. of Symbols*, 99), is ultimately the same as Merodach's. There is the same resemblance between ⋀, the thunderbolt, and ⋀, the Lycian and Carian E (Schliemann, 699).

[2] *Opera*, ed. Reisk, 1777, vol. vii. pp. 510-550. The various theories are that Ei means (1) "Thou art" (sc. the self-existent god), (2) "If" (expressive of the doubt of the suppliant), (3) "Five" (a mystic number).

[3] C. W. King, *The Gnostics*, fig. 26, p. 159. He identifies this Gnostic Є with " the Anchor of Seleucus," used as an emblem by the early Christians (Clem. Alex., *Pæd.*, iii. 11) (Id., p. 238).

[4] Schliemann, *op. cit.*, fig. 602, p. 435 ; fig. 278, and p. 363; and fig. 1958.

the Lithuanian thunder-god; our own thunder "bolt,"
(=arrow); Ger. *strahl-steine*;[1] the Runic Týr ⋏; the
"broad arrow," and much more which it were long to
tell.

NOTE C.—The solar character of the mythological conflict between the Dragon and his slayer is generally
transparently obvious.   Thus, in the Zend-Avesta, a
storm is represented as a battle for the light of
sovereignty, *hvarenô*, between Âtar, "Fire," the son of
Ahura, the Supreme God, and Azi Dahâka, "the fiendish
snake" or three-headed dragon;[2] while Mitra, who con-
quers Ahriman, the dark spirit of evil, is the god of
heavenly light, Pers. Mihr, the sun.[3]   The similar significance of the victory of Apollo over the monster Python
is brought out in these lines of Peele :

> "Sun, couldst thou shine, and see my love beset,
> And didst not clothe thy clouds in fiery coats,
> O'er all the heavens, with wingèd sulphur flames,
> As when thy beams, like mounted combatants,
> Battled with Python in the fallow'd lays?"[4]

NOTE D.—A belief in the intelligence or cunning of
the serpent is by no means confined to the Semitic races.
It is a part of the aboriginal folk-lore of the Algonkins
that the serpent is a master of magic and subtlety, and

---

[1] Grimm, *Teut. Myth.*, 179.

[2] *Zend-Avesta*, i. p. lxii.; ii. 293-4.

[3] Ibid., i. p. lx.

[4] *Edward I.* 1593. *Works*, 384. So St. George vanquishing the
Dragon was originally just the sun breaking through obstructing
clouds (D'Alviella, *Migration of Symbols*, 86); and Horus spearing
the infernal serpent bears the same meaning (see W. R. Cooper,
Serpent Myths of Ancient Egypt, 71, &c.).

hence dangerous to the human race ;[1] and Tamil writers
speak of the reptile as "a creature of deep searchings and
great secrecy."[2] Indeed, Greek *drakōn*, serpent, which
gives us our "dragon," means "the seeing one ;"[3] and the
same seems to be the etymological sense of Greek *ophis*,
serpent, connected with *optesthai*, to see.[4] The Nagas,
an Indian tribe, believe the serpent to be the symbol of
superior intelligence (*budh*), which conveyed the Vedas
into the deep and introduced letters into India (*Trans.
Asiatic Soc.*, ii. 563). Compare *supra*, p. 25. Similarly
pythōn, a name for the serpent in Greek, has been interpreted as meaning "the knowing" or "understanding
one" (πύθων, from root πυθ, επυθ-όμην, learn by inquiry,
know) ;[5] though Bochart prefers connecting it with
Heb. *pethen*, a species of serpent (*e.g.* Job xx. 16 ; Lxx.
δράκων), comparing late Heb. *pithān* (Syr. *pithun*), a
serpent, and *pithōm*, divination or necromancy by ven-
triloquism.[6] H. Spencer has shown that the snake or
serpent, from its habit of frequenting houses, has often
been regarded as a *revenant* or spirit of an ancestor still
attached to its old home and family.[7] It is accordingly
regarded with reverence and affection by the Russians[8]
and other Slavonic peoples, by the Dinka tribe of Central
Africa, who call it their "brother,"[9] and by the Moquis

[1] D. G. Brinton, *Essays of an Americanist*, 133.
[2] J. Roberts, *Orient. Illustrations*, 7.
[3] From the root *derk, dark*, to see; *cf.* late Gk. *drakos*, eyesight.
[4] Curtius, *Gk. Etymology*, ii. 63 ; Bochart, iii. 838.
[5] Ewald, *Revelation*, 227 ; Böttcher, *De Inferis*, 103.
[6] *Opera*, i. col. 383. [7] *Principles of Sociology* (3rd ed.), i. 326.
[8] Ralston, *Russ. Folk-Tales*, 115; Grimm, *Teut. Myth.*, 686 ; Tylor,
Prim. Cult., ii. 7, 217 ; Ralston, *Russ. Folk-Songs*, 124, 175.
[9] G. Schweinfurth, *Heart of Africa*, i. 158; Livingstone, &c.

of Arizona, who speak of it as their "father."[1]   From
thus standing in direct connection with the dead and the
underworld the serpent came to be considered as oracular
and capable of revealing the secrets of the spirit-world.[2]
The Ainus of Sakhalin, for instance, have a name for
demoniacal possession or, which in their view is the same
thing, madness, the literal meaning of which is "possession by snakes." With them snakes are incarnate
demons which affect human beings with bewitchment
or insanity.[3]   This serves to throw a new and interesting
light on a curious passage in the Acts of the Apostles
xvi. 16, where mention is made of a slave-girl at Philippi
whose power of divining or soothsaying was exploited
and made a gain of by a syndicate of proprietors.   She
is described as "having a *python* spirit" or "serpent
spirit."[4] Plutarch asserts that ventriloquists—*i.e.*, diviners
out of whom a spirit was believed to speak—were called
pythons;[5] and Tertullian says that the Magi used to
search out secret things by means of *pythonic* spirits (per
pythonicos spiritus).[6]   Arab dervishes in Palestine still
pretend to take counsel of serpents, which they carry
about with them, in working cures (Pierotti, *Customs*

---

[1] Spencer, *Sociology*, i. 797.

[2] Ewald (*Revelation*, 227), who brings the Greek *python*, the serpent,
and also spirit of divination, into connexion with the Vedic *Ahis
budhnjás*, "the serpent or the dragon of the abyss."

[3] E. D. Howard, *Life with Trans-Siberian Savages*, 194.

[4] All the best MSS. have πύθωνα πνεῦμα, not πύθωνος. Bp. Wordsworth has a long and interesting note, *in loco:* See Ovid, *Metamorph.* i.
438 *seq.*

[5] "Those spirits speaking within the bellies of possessed folks, such
as . . . . be now termed *pythons*" (Plutarch, *Morals*, tr. P. Holland,
1603, p. 1327).

[6] *De Anima.* cap. xxviii., *sub fin.*

and Traditions of Palestine, 49). Among the Dakotas of the New World as well as among the Arabs the one word serves for a serpent and a spirit (Brinton, *Myths of New World*, 114).

A reflex light is thus cast back upon the Hebrew term *nâchash*, to practise augury or divination, frequently used in the Old Testament (*e.g.*, Deut. xviii. 10; 2 Kings xvii. 17). The word is evidently akin to *nâchâsh*, a serpent, and denotes some species of ophiomancy; for, as Bochart remarks, serpents were believed by the ancients to inspire skill in soothsaying.[1]

NOTE E. (p. 57).—Mr. Gladstone observes that in the Homeric Poems Neptune, as ancestor of the rebellious Titans, and in other respects, has features characteristic of the Evil One (*Homer and the Homeric Age*, 1853, ii. 207). For Homeric traditions as to the fallen angels, see Id. ii. 164–167. Cf. Wisdom xiv. 6; Ecclus. xvi. 7; Baruch iii. 26–28.

NOTE F. (p. 66).—Tĕhôm (the abyss of destruction) has sometimes been used by modern Jews as a malicious play on the Christian word *dom*, a cathedral (von Bohlen, *Genesis*, i. 320). But for the final degradation of the word one must refer to Michel, *Sur l'Argot*, *s.v.* Thomas.

NOTE G. (p. 68).—So Shakspere:

"I can call spirits from the vasty deep."
1 *Henry IV*. iii. 1, 52.

---

[1] *Opera*, i. col. 21. In the Zend-Avesta all diseases are regarded as a kind of poisoning produced by the serpent (*cf.* Sansk. *drg-rischa*, "poison-looker," the serpent; Pictet, *Orig. Ind. Europ.*, i. 503), and consequently Thraðtaona, the serpent-slayer, is invoked to heal them (i. 219, ed. Darmestetor).

NOTE H. (p. 81).—What a recent writer, Professor Ihering, has said of our indebtedness to the Babylonians for the arts of civilisation may be extended with some reason to our religious obligations. "The inheritance of culture has descended from the Babylonians to the Indo-Europeans; and even as Hellas to-day survives in our art and science, and Rome in our law, so Babylon still lives in our culture. We owe her a very great deal more than is generally supposed" (*The Evolution of the Aryan*, trans. Drucker, 1897, p. 216). "The Aryans of Europe are indebted to the Semites for an incalculable amount of their civilisation, and, in many of our modern institutions, ancient Babylon survives to a very considerable extent" (Id. 225). It is strange and interesting to find the nations, long scattered abroad upon the face of all the earth, thus turning their faces back again to Babel, and finding there a point of union and kinship.

Printed by BALLANTYNE, HANSON & Co.
London & Edinburgh

A Selection from

MR. DAVID NUTT'S LIST

OF

PUBLICATIONS IN BIBLICAL ARCHÆOLOGY & SEMITIC PHILOLOGY

ADLER (MICHAEL, B.A., Senior Hebrew Master at the Jews Free School). THE ELEMENTS OF HEBREW GRAMMAR. With Exercises. Cloth. Net 1s. (1s. 2d. post free).

AMRAM (DAVID WERNER, M.A., Member of the Philadelphia Bar). THE JEWISH LAW OF DIVORCE ACCORDING TO BIBLE AND TAL-MUD, with some References to its Development in Post-Talmudic Times. Crown 8vo. Cloth. 6s.

DAVID NUTT, 270-271, STRAND, LONDON, W.C.

BARNSTEIN (HENRY, Ph.D.). THE TARGUM
OF ONKELOS TO GENESIS. A critical inquiry
into the value of the text exhibited by Yemen MSS.
compared with that of the European Recension,
together with specimen chapters of the Oriental text.
8vo. 1896. viii., 100 pp. Sewed. Net 3s. 6d.

THE SACRED BOOKS OF THE OLD TES-
TAMENT. A critical polychrome edition of the
Hebrew Text, with Notes. Edited by Prof. PAUL
HAUPT. 4to. Beautifully printed in colours. Already
issued (September 1897) :

> (17). JOB, edited by C. SIEGFRIED. 1893. 3s. 6d.
> (3). LEVITICUS, edited by Canon S. R. DRIVER.
> 1894. 2s. 6d.
> (8). SAMUEL, edited by K. BUDDE. 1894. 6s. 6d.
> (11). JEREMIAH, edited by C. H. CORNILL. 1895. 5s.
> (6). JOSHUA, edited by W. H. BENNETT. 1895. 3s.
> (14). PSALMS, edited by J. WELLHAUSEN. 1895. 6s.
> (20). CHRONICLES, edited by R. KITTEL. 1895. 6s.
> (18). DANIEL, edited by A. KAMPHAUSEN. 1896. 3s.
> (1). GENESIS, edited by C. J. BALL. 1896. 7s. 6d.
> ( ). EZRA and NEHEMIAH, edited by C. GUTHE.
> 1897.
> ( ). ISAIAH, edited by Canon T. K. CHEYNE. 1897.

COWPER (B. HARRIS). THE APOCRYPHAL GOS-
PELS, and Other Documents Relating to the History
of Christ. Translated from the Originals in Greek,
Syriac, Latin, &c. With Notes, Scriptural References,

and Prolegomena. Sixth Edition. Crown 8vo. cxii., 456 pages. Cloth. 5s.

. *The most complete and handy collection of New Testament Apocryphal literature extant.*

EVETTS (B. T. A.). COPTIC LITURGY. The Order of Baptism and the Order of Matrimony, translated from the MSS. 16mo. 1888. 61 pp. Hand-made paper. Sewed. 1s.

DAVIS (A.). THE HEBREW ACCENTS OF THE TWENTY-ONE BOOKS OF THE BIBLE. Crown 8vo. 1892. viii., 70 pp. Cloth. 3s. 6d.

DAVIS (JOHN D.). GENESIS AND SEMITIC TRADITION. 8vo. 1895. v., 150 pp. Illustrated. Cloth. 4s. 6d.

DIDACHE. THE DIDACHE, OR TEACHING OF THE TWELVE APOSTLES, restored to its original state from various sources. With Introduction, Translation, and Notes, by C. H. HOOLE. Demy 8vo. 1894. 70 pp. Net 2s. 6d.

FISKE (A. K.). THE JEWISH SCRIPTURES IN THE LIGHT OF THEIR ORIGIN AND HIS-TORY. Crown 8vo. 1896. xiv., 390 pp. Cloth. 5s.

. *A popular account of the subject from the advanced critical standpoint, based upon the latest research.*

DAVID NUTT, 270-271, STRAND, LONDON, W.C.

FRIPP (E. J.). THE COMPOSITION OF THE BOOK OF GENESIS. With English Text and Analysis. 12mo. 1892. 198 pp. Cloth. 4s.

GASTER (Rev. Dr. M.). THE SWORD OF MOSES. An ancient book of Magic from an unique (Hebrew.) Manuscript. With Introduction, Translation, an Index of Mystical Names, and a Facsimile. 8vo. 1896. lii., 35 pp. Sewed. Net 4s. 6d.

GREENBURG (W. H., PhD.). THE HAGGADAH ACCORDING TO THE RITE OF YEMEN, together with the Arabic-Hebrew Commentary. Published for the first time from MSS. of Yemen, with an Introduction, Translation, and Critical and Philological Notes. 8vo. 1896. lv., 80 pp. Sewed. Net 4s. 6d.

HARPER (W. R.). ELEMENTS OF HEBREW SYNTAX, by Inductive Method. 8vo. 1890. 177 pp. Cloth. 7s. 6d.

———— ELEMENTS OF HEBREW. 8vo. 1890. 200 pp. Cloth. 7s. 6d.

———— INTRODUCTORY HEBREW METHOD AND MANUAL. Sixth Edition. Crown 8vo. 1890. 176, 93 pp. Cloth. 6s.

DAVID NUTT, 270-271, STRAND, LONDON, W.C.

HARPER (W. R.). and WEIDNER (R. J.). AN
INTRODUCTORY NEW TESTAMENT GREEK
METHOD. (Text and Vocabulary of the Gospel of
John, List of Words and Elements of N.T. Greek
Grammar.) Crown 8vo. 1890. xx., 520 pp. Cloth.
7s. 6d.

JACOBS (JOSEPH). STUDIES IN BIBLICAL ARCHÆ-
OLOGY. Crown 8vo. 172 pp. Cloth. 3s. 6d.

> *Contents :* Recent Research in Biblical Archæology
> and Comparative Religion—Junior Right in
> Genesis—Totem Clans in the Old Testament—
> The Nethenim—The Indian Origin of Proverbs.

MARGOLIOUTH (G., M.A.). THE LITURGY OF
THE NILE. The Palestinian Syriac Text. Edited
from a Unique MS. in the British Museum, with a
Translation, Introduction, Vocabulary, and Two
Photo - lithographic Plates. Reprinted from the
" Journal of the Royal Asiatic Society." Net 5s.

MACDONALD (Rev. J. M., Houghton Syriac
Prizeman, Oxford). MASSILIA-CARTHAGO SAC-
RIFICE TABLETS OF THE WORSHIP OF
BAAL. Reproduced in Facsimile, Edited, Translated,
and compared with the Levitical Code. Crown 8vo.
Cloth. Net 3s. 6d.

TATTAM (Rev. H.). A COMPENDIOUS GRAMMAR
OF THE EGYPTIAN LANGUAGE, as contained

in the Coptic, Sahidic, and Bashmuric Dialects ; together with Alphabets and Numerals in the Hieroglyphic and Enchorial Characters.   Second Edition. 1863.   xxiv., 127 pp.   Six Plates.   Cloth.   Net 4s.

. *The simplest and most compendious Coptic grammar.*

WRIGHT (W.).   AN ARABIC READING BOOK. Part I.   The Texts.   8vo.   1870.   xxiv., 208 pp. Cloth.   Net 3s. 6d.

Contents : Stories of Arab Warriors—Historical Extracts Relating to Mohammed— Biographical Extracts—Geographical Extracts—Grammatical Extracts—Extracts from the Koran—Poems.

——— CONTRIBUTIONS TO THE APOCRYPHAL LITERATURE OF THE NEW TESTAMENT, Collected and Edited from Syriac Manuscripts in the British Museum, with an English Translation and Notes.   8vo.   1865.   xvi., 66 pp.   Cloth.   Net 4s.

Contents : The Protoevangelium Jacobi—The Gospel of Thomas—The Letters of Herod and Pilate—The History, Transitus, and Obsequies of the Virgin Mary.

. *Both of these works are nearly out of print.*

The Book of Enoch: Translated from the Editor's Ethiopic Text and Edited with an Enlarged Introduction, Notes and Indexes, Together with a Reprint of the Greek Fragments edited by R. H. Charles. *The Book of Enoch* was considered one of the most important books in early Christianity and was used widely. It seems to have predated everything in the New Testament, having been written, for the most part, in the second century BC (the first 36 chapters have been dated to approximately 175 BC). R. H. Charles, who translated the book, said, "the influence of *I Enoch* on the New Testament has been greater than that of all the other apocryphal and pseudepigraphical books put together." This book is undoubtedly the most important book left out of the Bible. This fact was acknowledged by editor R. H. Charles, so he researched the text with amazing detail. All his notes are included here, along with a list of every known translation of the texts and how they contributed to our knowledge. This is by far the most complete, thorough and scholarly edition which every serious researcher and student should have. In the early 1900s, after the book was first released, a number of Greek fragments were discovered. R. H. Charles used these newly discovered fragments along with Dillmann's earlier translation to create this invaluable, updated version in 1912. Five years later, in 1917, the slimmer edited version (ISBN 1-58509-019-0) replaced this thicker book, making it virtually impossible to find—until now. **ISBN 1-58509-080-8 • 448 pages • 6 x 9 • trade paper • $34.95**

The Book of the Secrets of Enoch, **translated from the Slavonic by W.R. Morfill. Edited, with Introduction and Notes by R. H. Charles.** For 1200 years this book was known to only a few people in Russia. When it was finally revealed to the world in 1892, it was announced that it was a Slavonic version of The Book of Enoch. This was wrong. Once translated, it was found that we have an entirely different book on and about Enoch, described, by the editor, as having no less value than the other book. This is a completely new and valuable pseudepigraph, one which every person should read who is interested in apocalyptic literature and the origins of Christianity. This particular book was read extensively by many separate Christian groups during the first three centuries, and it has left us today with many traces of its influence. It is now time to bring this book back into print so we may relearn its value to the world. This work was written in Egypt and we have determined that its author or original editor was a Hellenistic Jew. The Greek original has been lost to history, but the Slavonic text somehow survived. In its original Greek form it had a direct influence on the writers of the New Testament. This book was also referred to by Origen and used by the Church father, Irenaeus. It was read and considered valuable by the heretics of the day in addition to mainstream Christians. This may be one reason why it was excluded from the Bible. We hope this book will enlighten and inform those who are seeking the truth. **ISBN 1-58509-020-4 • 148 pages • 5 1/2 x 8 1/2 • trade paper • $13.95**

Enuma Elish: The Seven Tablets of Creation (in two volumes), **by L. W. King.** Subtitled: The Babylonian and Assyrian Legends Concerning the Creation of the World and of Mankind. The *Enuma Elish* is one of the oldest stories known to mankind. It is a story first written down by the ancient Sumerians thousands of years ago. As a one-time assistant in the Department of Egyptian and Assyrian Antiquities at the British Museum, L. W. King provides us with a qualified translation of the tablets that were originally written in cuneiform script. The *Enuma Elish* is receiving renewed interest from modern researchers delving into the origins of mankind, the earth, and the solar system. Over the centuries a copy ended up in the library at Nineveh in the 7th century BC, and was uncovered by archaeologists in the late 1800s. Written in cuneiform text and preserved on seven clay tablets, the entire story was called *The Seven Tablets of Creation.* After being translated the story revealed how the planets became aligned, how a cosmic catastrophe affected the earth, how mankind came upon the scene, and how the "gods" played a role in all of it. *The Seven Tablets of Creation* have had many profound implications since they were first discovered and published. They predate many parts of the Book of Genesis as well as other worldwide creation myths. Volume One includes this epic poem's English translation. It also includes information on parallels in Hebrew literature, the date and origin of the Babylonian creation legends, and more. **Vol 1: ISBN 1-58509-041-7 • 236 pages • 6 x 9 • trade paper • illustrated • $18.95. Vol 2: ISBN 1-58509-042-5 • 260 pages • 6 x 9 • trade paper • illustrated • $19.95**

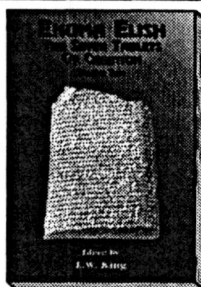

Of Heaven and Earth: Essays Presented at the First Sitchin Studies Day, edited by Zecharia Sitchin. ISBN 1-885395-17-5 • 164 pages • 5 1/2 x 8 1/2 • trade paper • illustrated • $14.95

God Games: What Do You Do Forever?, by Neil Freer. ISBN 1-885395-39-6 • 312 pages • 6 x 9 • trade paper • $19.95

Space Travelers and the Genesis of the Human Form: Evidence of Intelligent Contact in the Solar System, by Joan d'Arc. ISBN 1-58509-127-8 • 208 pages • 6 x 9 • trade paper • illustrated • $18.95

Humanity's Extraterrestrial Origins: ET Influences on Humankind's Biological and Cultural Evolution, by Dr. Arthur David Horn with Lynette Mallory-Horn. ISBN 3-931652-31-9 • 373 pages • 6 x 9 • trade paper • $17.00

Past Shock: The Origin of Religion and Its Impact on the Human Soul, by Jack Barranger. ISBN 1-885395-08-6 • 126 pages • 6 x 9 • trade paper • illustrated • $12.95

Flying Serpents and Dragons: The Story of Mankind's Reptilian Past, by R.A. Boulay. ISBN 1-885395-38-8 • 276 pages • 6 x 9 • trade paper • illustrated • $19.95

Triumph of the Human Spirit: The Greatest Achievements of the Human Soul and How Its Power Can Change Your Life, by Paul Tice. ISBN 1-885395-57-4 • 295 pages • 6 x 9 • trade paper • illustrated • $19.95

Mysteries Explored: The Search for Human Origins, UFOs, and Religious Beginnings, by Jack Barranger and Paul Tice. ISBN 1-58509-101-4 • 104 pages • 6 x 9 • trade paper • $12.95

Mushrooms and Mankind: The Impact of Mushrooms on Human Consciousness and Religion, by James Arthur. ISBN 1-58509-151-0 • 180 pages • 6 x 9 • trade paper • $16.95

Vril or Vital Magnetism, with an Introduction by Paul Tice. ISBN 1-58509-030-1 • 124 pages • 5 1/2 x 8 1/2 • trade paper • $12.95

The Odic Force: Letters on Od and Magnetism, by Karl von Reichenbach. ISBN 1-58509-001-8 • 192 pages • 6 x 9 • trade paper • $15.95

The New Revelation: The Coming of a New Spiritual Paradigm, by Arthur Conan Doyle. ISBN 1-58509-220-7 • 124 pages • 6 x 9 • trade paper • $12.95

The Astral World: Its Scenes, Dwellers, and Phenomena, by Swami Panchadasi. ISBN 1-58509-071-9 • 104 pages • 6 x 9 • trade paper • $11.95

Reason and Belief: The Impact of Scientific Discovery on Religious and Spiritual Faith, by Sir Oliver Lodge. ISBN 1-58509-226-6 • 180 pages • 6 x 9 • trade paper • $17.95

William Blake: A Biography, by Basil De Selincourt. ISBN 1-58509-225-8 • 384 pages • 6 x 9 • trade paper • $28.95

The Divine Pymander: And Other Writings of Hermes Trismegistus, translated by John D. Chambers. ISBN 1-58509-046-8 • 196 pages • 6 x 9 • trade paper • $16.95

Theosophy and The Secret Doctrine, by Harriet L. Henderson. Includes *H.P. Blavatsky: An Outline of Her Life,* by Herbert Whyte, ISBN 1-58509-075-1 • 132 pages • 6 x 9 • trade paper • $13.95

The Light of Egypt, Volume One: The Science of the Soul and the Stars, by Thomas H. Burgoyne. ISBN 1-58509-051-4 • 320 pages • 6 x 9 • trade paper • illustrated • $24.95

The Light of Egypt, Volume Two: The Science of the Soul and the Stars, by Thomas H. Burgoyne. ISBN 1-58509-052-2 • 224 pages • 6 x 9 • trade paper • illustrated • $17.95

The Jumping Frog and 18 Other Stories: 19 Unforgettable Mark Twain Stories, by Mark Twain. ISBN 1-58509-200-2 • 128 pages • 6 x 9 • trade paper • $12.95

The Devil's Dictionary: A Guidebook for Cynics, by Ambrose Bierce. ISBN 1-58509-016-6 • 144 pages • 6 x 9 • trade paper • $12.95

The Smoky God: Or The Voyage to the Inner World, by Willis George Emerson. ISBN 1-58509-067-0 • 184 pages • 6 x 9 • trade paper • illustrated • $15.95

A Short History of the World, by H.G. Wells. ISBN 1-58509-211-8 • 320 pages • 6 x 9 • trade paper • $24.95

The Voyages and Discoveries of the Companions of Columbus, by Washington Irving. ISBN 1-58509-500-1 • 352 pages • 6 x 9 • hard cover • $39.95

History of Baalbek, by Michel Alouf. ISBN 1-58509-063-8 • 196 pages • 5 x 8 • trade paper • illustrated • $15.95

Ancient Egyptian Masonry: The Building Craft, by Sommers Clarke and R. Engelback. ISBN 1-58509-059-X • 350 pages • 6 x 9 • trade paper • illustrated • $26.95

That Old Time Religion: The Story of Religious Foundations, by Jordan Maxwell and Paul Tice. ISBN 1-58509-100-6 • 220 pages • 6 x 9 • trade paper • $19.95

Jumpin' Jehovah: Exposing the Atrocities of the Old Testament God, by Paul Tice. ISBN 1-58509-102-2 • 104 pages • 6 x 9 • trade paper • $12.95

The Book of Enoch: A Work of Visionary Revelation and Prophecy, Revealing Divine Secrets and Fantastic Information about Creation, Salvation, Heaven and Hell, translated by R. H. Charles. ISBN 1-58509-019-0 • 152 pages • 5 1/2 x 8 1/2 • trade paper • $13.95

The Book of Enoch: Translated from the Editor's Ethiopic Text and Edited with an Enlarged Introduction, Notes and Indexes, Together with a Reprint of the Greek Fragments, edited by R. H. Charles. ISBN 1-58509-080-8 • 448 pages • 6 x 9 • trade paper • $34.95

The Book of the Secrets of Enoch, translated from the Slavonic by W. R. Morfill. Edited, with Introduction and Notes by R. H. Charles. ISBN 1-58509-020-4 • 148 pages • 5 1/2 x 8 1/2 • trade paper • $13.95

Enuma Elish: The Seven Tablets of Creation, Volume One, by L. W. King. ISBN 1-58509-041-7 • 236 pages • 6 x 9 • trade paper • illustrated • $18.95

Enuma Elish: The Seven Tablets of Creation, Volume Two, by L. W. King. ISBN 1-58509-042-5 • 260 pages • 6 x 9 • trade paper • illustrated • $19.95

Enuma Elish, Volumes One and Two: The Seven Tablets of Creation, by L. W. King. Two volumes from above bound as one. ISBN 1-58509-043-3 • 496 pages • 6 x 9 • trade paper • illustrated • $38.90

The Archko Volume: Documents that Claim Proof to the Life, Death, and Resurrection of Christ, by Drs. McIntosh and Twyman. ISBN 1-58509-082-4 • 248 pages • 6 x 9 • trade paper • $20.95

The Lost Language of Symbolism: An Inquiry into the Origin of Certain Letters, Words, Names, Fairy-Tales, Folklore, and Mythologies, by Harold Bayley. ISBN 1-58509-070-0 • 384 pages • 6 x 9 • trade paper • $27.95

The Book of Jasher: A Suppressed Book that was Removed from the Bible, Referred to in Joshua and Second Samuel, translated by Albinus Alcuin (800 AD). ISBN 1-58509-081-6 • 304 pages • 6 x 9 • trade paper • $24.95

The Bible's Most Embarrassing Moments, with an Introduction by Paul Tice. ISBN 1-58509-025-5 • 172 pages • 5 x 8 • trade paper • $14.95

History of the Cross: The Pagan Origin and Idolatrous Adoption and Worship of the Image, by Henry Dana Ward. ISBN 1-58509-056-5 • 104 pages • 6 x 9 • trade paper • illustrated • $11.95

Was Jesus Influenced by Buddhism? A Comparative Study of the Lives and Thoughts of Gautama and Jesus, by Dwight Goddard. ISBN 1-58509-027-1 • 252 pages • 6 x 9 • trade paper • $19.95

History of the Christian Religion to the Year Two Hundred, by Charles B. Waite. ISBN 1-885395-15-9 • 556 pages. • 6 x 9 • hard cover • $25.00

Symbols, Sex, and the Stars, by Ernest Busenbark. ISBN 1-885395-19-1 • 396 pages • 5 1/2 x 8 1/2 • trade paper • $22.95

History of the First Council of Nice: A World's Christian Convention, A.D. 325, by Dean Dudley. ISBN 1-58509-023-9 • 132 pages • 5 1/2 x 8 1/2 • trade paper • $12.95

The World's Sixteen Crucified Saviors, by Kersey Graves. ISBN 1-58509-018-2 • 436 pages • 5 1/2 x 8 1/2 • trade paper • $29.95

Babylonian Influence on the Bible and Popular Beliefs: A Comparative Study of Genesis I.2, by A. Smythe Palmer. ISBN 1-58509-000-X • 124 pages • 6 x 9 • trade paper • $12.95

Biography of Satan: Exposing the Origins of the Devil, by Kersey Graves. ISBN 1-885395-11-6 • 168 pages • 5 1/2 x 8 1/2 • trade paper • $13.95

The Malleus Maleficarum: The Notorious Handbook Once Used to Condemn and Punish "Witches", by Heinrich Kramer and James Sprenger. ISBN 1-58509-098-0 • 332 pages • 6 x 9 • trade paper • $25.95

Crux Ansata: An Indictment of the Roman Catholic Church, by H. G. Wells. ISBN 1-58509-210-X • 160 pages • 6 x 9 • trade paper • $14.95

Emanuel Swedenborg: The Spiritual Columbus, by U.S.E. (William Spear). ISBN 1-58509-096-4 • 208 pages • 6 x 9 • trade paper • $17.95

Dragons and Dragon Lore, by Ernest Ingersoll. ISBN 1-58509-021-2 • 228 pages • 6 x 9 • trade paper • illustrated • $17.95

The Vision of God, by Nicholas of Cusa. ISBN 1-58509-004-2 • 160 pages • 5 x 8 • trade paper • $13.95

The Historical Jesus and the Mythical Christ: Separating Fact From Fiction, by Gerald Massey. ISBN 1-58509-073-5 • 244 pages • 6 x 9 • trade paper • $18.95

Gog and Magog: The Giants in Guildhall; Their Real and Legendary History, with an Account of Other Giants at Home and Abroad, by F.W. Fairholt. ISBN 1-58509-084-0 • 172 pages • 6 x 9 • trade paper • $16.95

The Origin and Evolution of Religion, by Albert Churchward. ISBN 1-58509-078-6 • 504 pages • 6 x 9 • trade paper • $39.95

The Origin of Biblical Traditions, by Albert T. Clay. ISBN 1-58509-065-4 • 220 pages • 5 1/2 x 8 1/2 • trade paper • $17.95

Aryan Sun Myths, by Sarah Elizabeth Titcomb, Introduction by Charles Morris. ISBN 1-58509-069-7 • 192 pages • 6 x 9 • trade paper • $15.95

The Social Record of Christianity, by Joseph McCabe. Includes **The Lies and Fallacies of the Encyclopedia Britannica,** ISBN 1-58509-215-0 • 204 pages • 6 x 9 • trade paper • $17.95

The History of the Christian Religion and Church During the First Three Centuries, by Dr. Augustus Neander. ISBN 1-58509-077-8 • 112 pages • 6 x 9 • trade paper • $12.95

Ancient Symbol Worship: Influence of the Phallic Idea in the Religions of Antiquity, by Hodder M. Westropp and C. Staniland Wake. ISBN 1-58509-048-4 • 120 pages • 6 x 9 • trade paper • illustrated • $12.95

The Gnosis: Or Ancient Wisdom in the Christian Scriptures, by William Kingsland. ISBN 1-58509-047-6 • 232 pages • 6 x 9 • trade paper • $18.95

The Evolution of the Idea of God: An Inquiry into the Origin of Religions, by Grant Allen. ISBN 1-58509-074-3 • 160 pages • 6 x 9 • trade paper • $14.95

Sun Lore of All Ages: A Survey of Solar Mythology, Folklore, Customs, Worship, Festivals, and Superstition, by William Tyler Olcott. ISBN 1-58509-044-1 • 316 pages • 6 x 9 • trade paper • $24.95

Nature Worship: An Account of Phallic Faiths and Practices Ancient and Modern, by the Author of Phallicism with an Introduction by Tedd St. Rain. ISBN 1-58509-049-2 • 112 pages • 6 x 9 • trade paper • illustrated • $12.95

Life and Religion, by Max Muller. ISBN 1-885395-10-8 • 237 pages • 5 1/2 x 8 1/2 • trade paper • $14.95

Jesus: God, Man, or Myth? An Examination of the Evidence, by Herbert Cutner. ISBN 1-58509-072-7 • 304 pages • 6 x 9 • trade paper • $23.95

Pagan and Christian Creeds: Their Origin and Meaning, by Edward Carpenter. ISBN 1-58509-024-7 • 316 pages • 5 1/2 x 8 1/2 • trade paper • $24.95

The Christ Myth: A Study, by Elizabeth Evans. ISBN 1-58509-037-9 • 136 pages • 6 x 9 • trade paper • $13.95

Popery: Foe of the Church and the Republic, by Joseph F. Van Dyke. ISBN 1-58509-058-1 • 336 pages • 6 x 9 • trade paper • illustrated • $25.95

Career of Religious Ideas, by Hudson Tuttle. ISBN 1-58509-066-2 • 172 pages • 5 x 8 • trade paper • $15.95

Buddhist Suttas: Major Scriptural Writings from Early Buddhism, by T.W. Rhys Davids. ISBN 1-58509-079-4 • 376 pages • 6 x 9 • trade paper • $27.95

Early Buddhism, by T. W. Rhys Davids. Includes *Buddhist Ethics: The Way to Salvation?,* by Paul Tice. ISBN 1-58509-076-X • 112 pages • 6 x 9 • trade paper • $12.95

The Fountain-Head of Religion: A Comparative Study of the Principal Religions of the World and a Manifestation of their Common Origin from the Vedas, by Ganga Prasad. ISBN 1-58509-054-9 • 276 pages • 6 x 9 • trade paper • $22.95

India: What Can It Teach Us?, by Max Muller. ISBN 1-58509-064-6 • 284 pages • 5 1/2 x 8 1/2 • trade paper • $22.95

Matrix of Power: How the World has Been Controlled by Powerful People Without Your Knowledge, by Jordan Maxwell. ISBN 1-58509-120-0 • 104 pages • 6 x 9 • trade paper • $12.95

Cyberculture Counterconspiracy: A Steamshovel Web Reader, Volume One, edited by Kenn Thomas. ISBN 1-58509-125-1 • 180 pages • 6 x 9 • trade paper • illustrated • $16.95

Cyberculture Counterconspiracy: A Steamshovel Web Reader, Volume Two, edited by Kenn Thomas. ISBN 1-58509-126-X • 132 pages • 6 x 9 • trade paper • illustrated • $13.95

Oklahoma City Bombing: The Suppressed Truth, by Jon Rappoport. ISBN 1-885395-22-1 • 112 pages • 5 1/2 x 8 1/2 • trade paper • $12.95

The Protocols of the Learned Elders of Zion, by Victor Marsden. ISBN 1-58509-015-8 • 312 pages • 6 x 9 • trade paper • $24.95

Secret Societies and Subversive Movements, by Nesta H. Webster. ISBN 1-58509-092-1 • 432 pages • 6 x 9 • trade paper • $29.95

The Secret Doctrine of the Rosicrucians, by Magus Incognito. ISBN 1-58509-091-3 • 256 pages • 6 x 9 • trade paper • $20.95

The Origin and Evolution of Freemasonry: Connected with the Origin and Evolution of the Human Race, by Albert Churchward. ISBN 1-58509-029-8 • 240 pages • 6 x 9 • trade paper • $18.95

The Lost Key: An Explanation and Application of Masonic Symbols, by Prentiss Tucker. ISBN 1-58509-050-6 • 192 pages • 6 x 9 • trade paper • illustrated • $15.95

The Character, Claims, and Practical Workings of Freemasonry, by Rev. C.G. Finney. ISBN 1-58509-094-8 • 288 pages • 6 x 9 • trade paper • $22.95

The Secret World Government or "The Hidden Hand": The Unrevealed in History, by Maj.-Gen., Count Cherep-Spiridovich. ISBN 1-58509-093-X • 270 pages • 6 x 9 • trade paper • $21.95

The Magus, Book One: A Complete System of Occult Philosophy, by Francis Barrett. ISBN 1-58509-031-X • 200 pages • 6 x 9 • trade paper • illustrated • $16.95

The Magus, Book Two: A Complete System of Occult Philosophy, by Francis Barrett. ISBN 1-58509-032-8 • 220 pages • 6 x 9 • trade paper • illustrated • $17.95

The Magus, Book One and Two: A Complete System of Occult Philosophy, by Francis Barrett. ISBN 1-58509-033-6 • 420 pages • 6 x 9 • trade paper • illustrated • $34.90

The Key of Solomon The King, by S. Liddell MacGregor Mathers. ISBN 1-58509-022-0 • 152 pages • 6 x 9 • trade paper • illustrated • $12.95

Magic and Mystery in Tibet, by Alexandra David-Neel. ISBN 1-58509-097-2 • 352 pages • 6 x 9 • trade paper • $26.95

The Comte de St. Germain, by I. Cooper Oakley. ISBN 1-58509-068-9 • 280 pages • 6 x 9 • trade paper • illustrated • $22.95

Alchemy Rediscovered and Restored, by A. Cockren. ISBN 1-58509-028-X • 156 pages • 5 1/2 x 8 1/2 • trade paper • $13.95

The 6th and 7th Books of Moses, with an Introduction by Paul Tice. ISBN 1-58509-045-X • 188 pages • 6 x 9 • trade paper • illustrated • $16.95

Lightning Source UK Ltd.
Milton Keynes UK
UKOW02f1857190815

257215UK00001B/111/P